THE STEPPE IN HISTORY

THE STEPPE IN HISTORY

Essays on a Eurasian Fringe

SUCHANDANA CHATTERJEE

Maulana Abul Kalam Azad
Institute of Asian Studies
Kolkata

MANOHAR
2010

First published 2010

ISBN 978-81-7304-882-1

Published by
Ajay Kumar Jain *for*
Manohar Publishers & Distributors
4753/23 Ansari Road, Daryaganj,
New Delhi 110 002

Printed at
Salasar Imaging Systems
Delhi 110 035

Contents

Preface

The steppe deserves to be treated as a special category in Eurasian history, not because of its Russianized environment but because of its Asiatic image. The present study deals with several impressions that indicate an intermingling of opinions about the steppe. It analyses two important facets of steppe historiography—the Kazakh domain and the Siberian domain, highlighting features that have relevance outside the Russian mould. The purpose has been to integrate intertwined histories of the two domains and indicate continuities and discontinuities of two overlapping strands of history-writing, Soviet and post-Soviet. The representation of the steppe in Soviet and post-Soviet literature is therefore an important component of this study.

SUCHANDANA CHATTERJEE

Acknowledgements

I am grateful to the Maulana Abul Kalam Azad Institute of Asian Studies for supporting my research on regional histories of the Eurasian steppe. I would like to thank the institute for providing me support during study trips and international conferences abroad as well as within India.

I acknowledge with gratitude the support of the institute's director, Prof. H.S. Vasudevan in every aspect of my research. As my teacher he has guided me academically and has critically examined my work. His research ideas have helped me to revise my draft, with special attention to Tsarist, Soviet and post-Soviet perspectives.

I am also grateful to Prof. Jayanta Kumar Ray, Chairman of the Institute for encouraging research on my area of interest.

I take this opportunity to thank my colleagues at the institute whose professional inputs have helped me in numerous ways. The pleasant corridor talks were a welcome break during the most crucial stage of writing this manuscript. Special thanks to Kausik who helped me with material search on Owen Lattimore.

I also acknowledge the support of the library team of the institute and thank Sandip Sarkar for helping me in my search for material on the steppe.

Special thanks to Diloram Karomat for helping me to learn Kazakh in Kolkata.

Interaction with our Siberian collaborators in Novosibirsk, Ulan Ude and Irkutsk has also helped me immensely in my work. The Institute of History, Novosibirsk, and the Institute of Mongolian, Buddhist and Tibetan Studies (IMBT), Ulan Ude, have been extremely cooperative and I am overwhelmed by their enthusiasm about my work. I recall with gratitude the hospitality of Prof. Lamin and his team in Novosibirsk and for gifting our institute a wealth of material on Siberia which I could utilize for my present project. Prof. Boris Bazarov, Prof. Marina Baldano and Prof. Viktor I. Dyatlov have introduced me to the expanding domain of Siberian Studies.

I acknowledge with gratitude the names of Uyama Tomohiko, Kimitaka Matsuzato, Norihiro Naganawa, David Wolff and others at the Slavic Research Centre, Hokkaido, with whom I had interacted closely during my brief visit in 2007 as an invited speaker. I am grateful to Joachim Otto Habeck and his Siberian Studies team as well as other senior scholars at Max Planck Institute of Social Anthropology (Halle) for inviting me to give a talk at their centre and for giving me useful suggestions about contemporary research and field studies on Siberia. I feel encouraged by their suggestions about combining methodologies of history with field-based observations. I specially thank my friend Judith Beyer for being my guide in Halle's research environment. The friendly gestures of the KISI team in Almaty and Guljanat Kurmangalieva, Konuralp Ercilasun, Ilhan Sahin of Bishkek-Manas University will remind me always of Central Asia's hospitality. The ambience in Ankara and Tsukuba is something I can never forget.

For alternative views on the Altai as a Siberian region and the dialectics of Inner Asia and Outer Asia, I remain grateful to Vladimir Boyko, a senior historian of Altai State University.

Special thanks are due to Stephane Dudoignon for indulging me in collaborative projects like *Abstracta Iranica* and *Central Asian Reader*. A mere 'thank you' for Forouz may not be enough to express my deep gratitude for her hospitality in Paris.

I am also fortunate to have consulted Allen Frank in Tsukuba whose expertise about Islamic historiography is perhaps well known. His insights about Islamic textual sources in Kazakhstan have been useful for my research.

Home is where the heart belongs. Not many words can express my feelings for my family that has learnt to tolerate my absentee status. Sukalyan always guided me to accept research as a challenge. My children, Som and Mimi are my life support. It was wonderful to share some light moments with them whenever I felt exhausted with work.

SUCHANDANA CHATTERJEE

Introduction

THE ARGUMENT

The present study seeks to study the steppe as a special category in Eurasian history. The purpose of this venture is to take into account multiple dimensions of steppe history which otherwise tend to get framed in a discourse about colonial transformation. The study intend to gauge the extent and control of the Turko-Mongol domain stretching from Hungary in the east to Lake Baikal in the west—a region that was transformed from a magnificent citadel of political authority of the three Mongol hordes to a post-Mongol dispensation that was dominated by Tatar tribes and Cossack riders who entrenched themselves subsequently in a settler-dominated Russian fort area. So, the basic idea of the steppe is a region that was filled with grasslands, barbaric raiders and horsemen and distanced from the locus of imperial power. It is only recently that the steppe, a continental landmass on the south of Russia that overlaps with Mongolian and Chinese borderlands, has received fair treatment as an interactive space. While it is still very difficult to pinpoint writings that deal with the steppe as a social phenomenon, one can still cite a few works that questioned earlier formats.

Here, we are concerned with both Soviet and post-Soviet approaches, the former expressing a predictable set of opinions and the latter questioning that set of opinions. Scholars for a long time focused on the southern rim of the Russian empire but were not uninterested in 'competing empires'. They were apparently fascinated with the aspect of Russia's Islamic subjects in the Caucasus, Tatar regions and Central Asia.[1] Some were also inspired by the dynastic histories and focused on the early history of the steppe. Recently, however, the steppe's nomadic environment that had significant contacts with the sedentary surroundings has received considerable attention. Such works are stylistically different from those written during the Soviet era. In the Soviet period too, writing about the non-Russian people was a serious enterprise but that scholarship was guided strictly by the party doctrine and borderlands history became the virtual preserve of academics who were committed to write the history of the heartland. This professional commitment began to disintegrate during *perestroika* but it really took some time for scholars to consider borderlands' history as crucially important to Eurasia. It was only in the late 1980s that a significant change took place and the interest about Russia's national minorities regained focus.[2]

The study takes into account the old and new formats of borderlands' history of the Russian empire and examines the perceptions about the steppe not merely as an imperial fringe but also as a zone of competition among tribal chieftains of the Middle and Small Hordes, the Khan of Kokand and others with fragmented loyalty to the Golden Horde. In imperial records, especially after 1891 when the steppe's administrative structure was formalized, the tendency was to highlight the distinctive features of the region, whether it was in terms of geography, ethnography or political entity. In *Entsiklopedicheski Slovar'* (1897), for instance, the emphasis was on the geographical setting of South Russia and the historical landmarks of the region as Russian colonial settlers started their intrusions in the sixteenth century. The steppe, according to the Slovar', is *sukhia prostranstva* (dry surrounding) that is very distinct from the forest zone or the tundra in the higher latitudes or the desert surroundings in the lower latitudes.[3] So, on the one hand, the steppe grasslands converge with the black earth (*chernozem*) soil of Hungary in the west to the Irkutsk-Mongolian plateau in the east. The steppe region's overlapping territory with mountain regions like the Altai and desert regions like the Gobi is also to be considered. According to ethnographic mapping, the steppe region comprised of the Russian settlers, Turko-Mongol tribal communities belonging to the Middle Horde, Siberian Tatars and Siberian Cossacks stretching as far as the Far East.[4] Political authority was fragmented among the tribal chiefs the Great and Middle Hordes, especially after the Russians had established military defence lines in the seventeenth and eighteenth centuries in the Akmolinsk and Semipalatinsk oblasts (province) of Kazakhstan, the Semirechie up to the Ishim and Irtysh rivers in western Siberia. The Russians set up a chain of forts that stretched from Omsk, Semipalatinsk, Ust-Kamenogorsk up to the Yenisei tract and controlled parts of the steppe west of Tomsk (e.g. Baraba and Kulunda). The Russians secured this entire territory largely through Cossack control that demonstrated the specialized defense mechanism of a group of people with different ethnic backgrounds who helped to expand and consolidate an imperial system in the steppe rim of Siberia. What began as Russian exploratory missions combined with a strategy of trade expansion via the Kazakh and Kalmyk territory in order to reach the Persian and Indian markets were gradually converted into more concrete measures for gaining imperial control mainly by becoming extra-dependent on local forces like the Cossacks and the Kazakhs and through the development of a colonial apparatus that included the Kazakhs of the Middle and the Elder Hordes. According to imperial records, therefore, the steppe's unruly landscape, political entity and ethnographic component defined the character of Russia's southern and south-eastern border. The element of distinction is clear here—the north of Russia comprising wooded forests was a different environment compared to the south or east of Russia which is Asiatic Russia. In imperialist perception, the region had a different natural environment and lay at the edge of imperial control. The Russians never meddled with the nomads of the region and Russian advancement into the region was fairly cautious, at least till the sixteenth century. But the advancement also reflected a pattern—the system of control that began with the trading pursuits of Novgorod merchants eventually redefined itself as a military-cum-administrative power apparatus along the Siberian defence line that was sustained by Cossack regiments. So, basically it is a study of human control of an environment that was so exclusive. It is this particular aspect of environment study that has rendered the steppe a special case in Russian historical studies and a special category of frontier research. Studies in Russian historical geography have indicated the relevance of environmental determinism and frontier geography in determining the causes and character of imperial control that range between scouting missions, farming activities and settlement initiatives to actual military-cum-administrative control.[5] So the search for the Black Earth zone propelled a surge of Russian peasant settlements up to the Kazakh steppe—a fact that is supported by *Entsiklopedicheski Slovar'*. So when we speak of the steppe space, we refer to a variety of regions—the farming settlements of the Kazakh upland that are well-connected by the Trans-Siberian Railroad, the military settlements or the *voevody* that extend up to the Yenisei *gubernia* as well as the 'steppe outskirts' or *razbrosanie* that extend beyond Irkutsk and Trans-Baikal up to Mongolia in the east including its lower hilly slopes, passes and lower reaches of the Gobi Desert. Encyclopaedic categories, namely *Steppe* and *Sibir*, reveal the significance of the river-valleys in the eastern and western ends of the steppe that encompass the variety of ethnographic tribes of Turkic, Mongol and Finnish origin, referred to as the *inorodetsy* (aliens). Even as we take note of the colonial connotation of the Eurasian steppe, we ought to remember that it is the inter-tribal relations of eastern and south-eastern Siberia that actually determined the nature of that Asiatic space of Russia. For instance, we have the Buryat Mongols in the Lake Baikal area sharing space with the Tungus tribes as well as with the Yenisei Kyrgyz of the Krasnoyarsk region. So the eastern reaches of the Siberian khanate (concentrated on the Irtysh River) that include the Tatars as well as the non-Tatars, i.e. the Tomsk and Tobolsk Tatars and the Mongols and Tungus groups of Buryatia, Irkutsk *gubernia* (governor generalate) and Trans-Baikal actually denote the steppe space of Asiatic Russia.[6]

This character of Asiatic Russia is the subject matter of post-Soviet depictions of steppe history.[7] The traditional image of the steppe as a vast continental grassland and a zone of control of Turko-Mongol nomadic warriors competing with each other since the ninth century AD and challenged by the colonial dispensation of the nineteenth century has been replaced by images of a vibrant steppe ecumene. The present study is concerned with how this ecumene has been represented in the twentieth century. The study bears in mind the fact that the steppe has always been studied from a Russian angle and hence the colonial dispensation is central to discussions about the steppe's military history. Within that format too, opinions have differed. Sometimes, it is not impossible to detect the inside story. The present study is more concerned with the inside story that surfaced in the scattered material about 'people's history', especially in the case of Kazakhstan and Siberia. Early Soviet reflections about people's history are evident in M. Viatkin's account of 'voices' in Kazakh society—rebelliousness of feudal lords and tribal leaders like Iset Kotybarov and Kenesary Kasymov, elite intellectuals and their imperial missions (e.g. Chokan Valikhanov) and common people or the working class (who participated in the 1941 war for victory of the Fatherland).[8] In Viatkin's outlay of what appears to be a Kazakh narrative, the people's mood gets prominence.

The reckoning of people's history became a sensitive issue in Siberia in the 1990s. Prior to that, Siberian people's role was not a subject of great relevance especially among the St.

Petersburg literati. The five-volume *Istoriya Sibiri* highlights Siberia's progression from an archaic domain to a Sovietized environment in the 1960s but the voluminous texts are scanty in details about the indigenous communities. The lapses were overcome when Siberian historians started portraying the region, its role and place as a region that was resonating with the socio-cultural idealism of the *oblastniki*, *a* region that was the Russian resource base and became the credo of the liberation movement popularized by N.M. Yadrintsev in his *Sibir' kak koloniya* (1882), a region that was idealized by émigré nationalists seeking an international platform in the early twentieth century and a region that ceased to become an alternative because of divided political interests. Despite this factionalism, we get the picture of the *oblastniki* as an insider. What is outstanding is the intellectual maturity *oblastniki*. Outsiders like James Forsyth also felt the pulse of the Siberians. In his account of the people's history of Siberia, Forsyth wrote a guidebook about Russia's people in the North.[9] The attempt was to compile facts and figures into one single volume about the indigenous people of Siberia who had Tatar, Mongol and Turkic lineage. He is no Soviet writer who compiled a database about Siberia's integration into a state-managed apparatus or the prestigious urban circuit of Siberia. Igor Naumov's *History of Siberia* (RoutledgeCurzon, 2006) is just an addition to the translated English-language material on Siberia. Because of the lack of analysis, this book is one minor attachment to the book world on Siberia. In my study, I try to bring together some of these varied impressions about a region which despite its *presence* in Soviet directories and high profile historical surveys, has not been studied carefully as a steppe locale. If we treat these impressions on a mass scale, we are bound to be struck by the graded perceptions of a Siberian or Kazakh history. On the one hand there is a colonial hangover. On the other hand, there is a rather tangential treatment of Siberia's 'living history' and her links with Central Asian and Mongolian borderlands tend to get undermined. What is clear is Russia's *presence* in Asia but what is unclear is the extent of that Asian space or how is that Asian space represented both before and after the disintegration.

The present study encompasses the broad interest about Siberia, not restricting itself to the myth factor that has dominated most of the literature on the region. Recent reappraisals of the Mongol phenomenon in steppe history which highlight not only a pre-Tsarist Mongol setting[10] but also a series of internal phenomena that were treated rather narrowly as 'feudal', 'reactionary', 'bourgeois' or 'counter-revolutionary' also provide a new historical framework.

The study takes into consideration the spatial unit—a diverse terrain extending over 4,000 km of territory with large stretches of open grasslands, marshes and lakes as well as high plateaus and forests, stretching from Hungary in the west to Vladivostok in the east, encompassing a Kazakh nomadic belt that was dotted with Cossack military outposts and merging with south Siberian urban locales along the Trans-Siberian railway route. In the present study, the steppe's territoriality is not the crucial element. More significant is the *spatial history*, i.e. the civilizational paradigm of a Eurasian space with major focus on shared histories, shared cultures and shared territories that have led to a 'rediscovery' of Russia's presence in Asia. The prime focus is not on frontiers as peripheries or frontiers as the outer domain of an expansionist empire but as provinces and regions with experiences of development and contact with metropolitan centres like Moscow and St. Petersburg. The focus is also on the frontier *initatics* of the Kazakhs, Cossacks and the Siberians who were the autochthonous people of the Russian Empire and have retained a distinct socio-political culture. The discussion is not only about the steppe as a military frontier where raiders and military commanders exercised their might but as a dynamic human environment which became a significant area of research in the field of historical geography. The impact of geographical and economic resources on the environment and the specific historical context within which transformation took place through railways and peasant settlements has been referred to. Also significant are the nomadic environment in south Russia and the Kazakh resilience in a colonial environment—the subject of Viatkin's study. In Viatkin's survey, the political fragmentation of the Chingizid elite in the thirteenth century had not displaced individual Khans who were unwieldy and were able to garner local support for their resistance movements in the steppe. Some of them not only had their own groups of supporters or loyal servants (*tulenguts*) to carry out the raids on Tsarist settlements but also used intra-tribal differences to their own advantage. Such caucus groups among the Kazakh Khans and their ability to uphold the Khan lineage in specific ways is the subject matter of restoration writings of the post-Soviet period. Awkward deals through tribal contacts were put to use by leaders like Abul Khair, Srym Batyr and Kenesary Kasymov.

THE SUBJECT

The study takes into consideration new methodological interpretations on the subject of the frontier. Notions of the frontier as 'a colonial other' have been replaced by complimentary views of resilience, vitality, sustainability, reciprocation, collaboration and governance of a Eurasian fringe. There is an attempt to reconsider the imperial setting and go beyond the frame of unequal binary relationships between the nomad and the settler, the civilized and the barbarian, the colonizer and the colonized, the urban and the rural. Within the format of 'regionology' and 'imperiology' are discussed wide-angle perspectives about a region that was once part of the imperial apparatus and has now secured a new image of a human habitat that transforms itself into a social environment. An array of opinions about a virtually transformed landscape has made its way into the realm of history, historical geography, sociology, social anthropology and 'critical' International Relations studies.

A crucial aspect of the new research is its comparative framework and the obvious comparison is Soviet and post-Soviet approaches towards regional history. During the Soviet period, the writings were based on the 'periodization of history' model which differed from post-Soviet views about social environment that influenced history-writing. History-writing as an 'inherited tradition' has been treated very recently by Arup Banerji in his retrospective analysis of Soviet works.[11] Banerji's analysis of Soviet intellectual space is influenced by the writings of Anatole G. Mazour, the non-partisan historian of the Cold War period whose dossiers on Russian and Soviet historiographical traditions are special because of their in-depth analysis and wide coverage.[12] Mazour studied the professional environment of Soviet historians who were commissioned to write on specific subjects. There was a reformulation of 'the party line' during the post-Stalinist phase and factual evidence became the *alma mater* of Soviet periodicals and journals.

There was a shift of methodology at every stage of 'historical enquiry' in the Soviet Union. The disciplining of history by the Communist Party was a recurrent issue and historians were 'instructed' to provide factual representations of history on almost every aspect that the Communist ideologues could think about. The study of sources (*istochnikovedenie*) had wide appeal and state academies played a vital role in popularizing the tradition of learning and re-learning historical sources on matters related to feudal development, commercial growth, demographic patterns, and so on. The role of the Soviet publishing world in disseminating ideas about socialist re-construction in Siberia and the patronage of party-supported journals (*Voprosy Istorii* and *Istoriya SSSR*) indicate the Soviet milieu which influenced the writings of that specific period.[13] Mazour and Banerji have reflected on the Soviet perspective—the perspective about a region in the making. This perspective hinted at the socialist mind that was ambitious about the programmes that were launched to tame the wild nature in Siberia. Soviet accounts demonstrate how Soviet daredevils, employed and inspired by the Soviet state, tried to overcome nature's odds in the taiga and tundra.[14] As 'primitive communists', the Siberians became the 'leap to the future' programme's best beneficiaries. At the end of the war in 1945,

Soviet urban planners shifted their focus to the Urals and Siberia. Since the 1950s, cities in the east of the Ural Mountains became the loci of fast-growing population and industry, and many Siberian cities became major urban centres for the first time. Statistics reveal their growth from small towns to imperial outposts during the tsarist era to cities of several hundred thousand and even more during the Soviet period.[15] Soviet urbanization in the Eurasian steppe, particularly to the east of the Urals became a subject of historical inquiry.

Space is a category of analysis in post-Soviet writings about the region. A recent review of the 'terrain' turns the spotlight on space as a discursive site. Spatial history has obtained a new rhythm in the writings of *Kritika*, a scholarly journal on Russian and Eurasian history that elegantly treats space as a human environment. What differentiates this genre of writing from the specialized field of historical geography of the 1960s, 1970s and the 1980s is the understanding of spatial surrounding and the 'shared critical interest in the *interaction* of space with human agency'.[16] Such writings have not only reinvigorated the domain of Russian historical geography but have also refined the earlier prejudiced views of British historians about Soviet scholarship.[17] Experiencing a particular space and 'working through the eyes' model has set the tone of new research. 'The sharpening of spatial optics' through experiences of travel has been specifically addressed by post-Soviet writers. Several examples about the 'sighting of space' model could be cited and the South Asian experience is of special relevance here. The travel experiences of the Indian scholar-traveller Rahula Sankrityayana in the Soviet Union in the 1940s indicates his sojourn to the socialist world that brought him in direct contact with the region on its threshold.[18]

The idea of space as a human environment is however not an entirely new concept and pioneering studies in this direction were made by Frederick Jackson Turner in 1893 and Owen Lattimore in 1928. The latter's observations in the 1930s and the 1940s constituted the basis of what has been recognized as the Lattimorian tradition. While Turner referred to the American frontier as a progressive frontier, Lattimore spoke about the adaptability of frontiers in Inner Asia that converged with Mongolian or Russian frontiers. The adaptability process was linked to human movements along these frontiers which gradually assumed global focus. The methods of Lattimore's analysis are applied to a vast range of spatial arenas: to the borderlands of China, to Japan, to Europe and America and to the world as a whole. In its overall attempt to summarize the range of scholarship about the Eurasian steppe, the present study refers to Turner and Lattimore's frontier concepts and the continuity of their traditions till the present day.

Central to all these discussions about a Eurasian fringe is the steppe territory. Most of these discussions have taken place rather predictably within the framework of Russian colonialism. The Soviet directories *Istoriya Sibiri* (1968) and *Istoriya Kazakhstana* are impressive accounts of state-sponsored projects and have a set framework—i.e. denouncement of 'feudal peculiarities' and praise of Soviet reconstruction projects. The style of writing is also predictable—periods of history and a progression of events from feudalism to communism via capitalism. The steppe domain's nomadic environment exhibiting strong links with neighbouring Turco-Tatar-Mongol khanates was denounced as feudal. There was reflection on agents of progress and state patronage received fair treatment. In the post-Soviet period, the emphasis was on the social setting rather than centralized planning.

THE ESSAYS

In this work there are three main essays that deal with the continuities of dominant historiography and departures from the traditional model. These are:

1. The Steppe as Frontier
2. The Kazakh Story
3. The Siberian Domain

The first essay deals with the qualitative leap in representations of Eurasian history—whereby frontiers and borderlands are treated as interactive spaces and not as peripheries that succumbed to imperial control. There is an attempt to study the expanded domain in Eurasia's borderland studies, focusing not only on the dominant constellations of the Russian empire but also on the vibrant mechanism that were integral to that imperial setup. The essay begins with a discussion of the conceptualization of the term 'frontier' by Turner in 1893 and a critique of the Turnerian position by his contemporaries as well his rival camp represented by the disciples of another pioneering frontier spokesman of the early twentieth century, Owen Lattimore. Turner's concept of the mobility of the American frontier in the western direction was a reflection of his convictions of American-style development and a contrast to Lattimore's concept of China's vibrant frontiers in the east.

The second essay deals with the Kazakh 'conscience' in the post-disintegration period that defined the spatial arena of what has been called 'the Kazakh story'. This conscience was based on a retrieval of Kazakh history and was reflected in the priorities of research in the post-Soviet period. These priorities were: (a) concern for the Russian past, (b) affiliation to tribal genealogical patterns, and (c) premises of Kazakh intellectualism. The subject of Russian 'transformation' became a tricky issue, especially because of the internal pressures and ruptures that became more prominent as the Kazakhs were desperately trying to negotiate with the imperial authorities over collective rights (land) and individual rights (cattle). The insoluble nature of these disputes and the stringent nature of steppe statutes is a factor that soured relations between the Kazakhs and the Russians. This aspect of unequal relationship between the two sides that set the tone of rupture in the Kazakh society has been treated in post-Soviet literature. The colonial environment also offered a unique opportunity to the Kazakh intellectuals to express themselves as a social stratum with a feeling of responsibility. Through their interactive newspaper

Dala Walayitining Gazeti (1882-1902), the Kazakh intellectuals tried to make their people more conscious about the implications of administrative statutes. Their newspaper was also a platform for establishing a concord with the imperial authorities. This interactive social milieu was one aspect of the Kazakh story that has received a wide coverage. The Kazakh story also revolves round diverse reactions regarding Kazakh 'destiny'—dissent and rebellion of Khan Kenesary Kasymov in 1834-47 in order to reassert land rights, the genesis of a secular world-view among educated Kazakhs, the emergence of the movement for *Alash* (unity) and the beginnings of the Alash Orda movement (1905-17) that imbibed ideals of political autonomy. With such fresh insights there has been a tendency to review power relationships in the steppe. There were thus twists in tale and Soviet and post-Soviet Kazakh historiographies have dealt with episodic aspects of Kazakh history.

The third essay pinpoints aspects that have created euphoria among Siberia's historians today and resurrected Siberia's image as the land of the future. The first aspect is Siberia's economic performance that is specially related to Siberians' commercial activities in the Tsarist period and the Soviets' zeal about agrarian reform and urban development that put Siberia on a new pedestal. The legacy of commercial development in Siberia is traced back to the eleventh-century tribute-exacting fur traders of Novgorod who competed with local traders of the Komi basin. Subsequent developments like the sixteenth-century entrepreneurial activity of the Stroganov merchants and others in Omsk, Tomsk, Barnaul, Novonikolaevsk (Novosibirsk) and Yeniseinsk and a series of Russian expeditions on the Pacific littoral in the nineteenth century gave Siberia its special status as a resource belt. This resource status of Siberia turned into N.M. Yadrintsev's tool of attack against the commercialization of the region in the nineteenth century. Yadrintsev's ideology defined *oblastnichestvo* (regionalism) as the regionalist alternative in Siberia in the twentieth century that has acquired a lot of attention in the aftermath of the Siberian Accord (1990). It is the internationalization of *oblastnichestvo* that has made the biggest difference in Siberia's history. The Siberian saga is also represented by the dominant narrative about the transformation of a region through Tsarist enterprises like the Trans-Siberian Railroad and the peasant resettlement policy. The railroad became a metaphor of land connectivity which inspired writers of the post-Soviet generation. Institutional patronage was a historical tradition in Siberia and Siberia's historians have devoted special attention to this aspect of institutional support for basic research about Siberian history. These aspects represent the saga of Siberia that is being retold by those who appreciate the region's history in exclusion from its Russian framework.

SOURCES AND FINDINGS

Research on these aspects have been text-based and opinion-based. A comparative study of Soviet and post-Soviet accounts has led to an understanding of the emphasis in each period. In order to understand the essence of the literature specific to the steppe, subjects like frontier studies and the relevance of the steppe domain in frontier discourse, intellectualism among the Kazakhs, *oblastnichestvo* in Siberia have been studied partially through an analysis of original writings and partially through an analysis of the *interpretations* of these writings or allied subjects. Original writings convey an idea about the hypothesis, impressions and retrospection of a particular period. In this category is the thesis of Turner as well as Lattimore's pioneering articles,[19] Viatkin's 'people survey'[20] and the Sibiriaks' deconstruction of Yadrintsev's *Sibir' kak koloniya.*[21] In the first essay I have referred to the theoretical premises of the term frontier, specifically using Turner's paradigm on the American frontier and Owen Lattimore's popular dictum on Inner Asian frontiers. Their prescriptions unfold the frontier as an interactive space. To get an image of the interactive space that Siberia represents, I have studied the travel writings of the Indian scholar-traveller Rahul Sankrityayana and the Russian painter Nicholas Roerich.[22] The former, a diehard disciple of socialism, visited the Soviet Union in the 1940s to get an idea of the socialist reconstruction that was taking place there. Roerich on the other hand visited the Altai in the 1920s. The surrealism of the region, the beauty and bounties of the land, the civilizational component were attractive to the artistic traveller but were considered to be endangered species because of the post-revolutionary political turmoil in the Inner Asian borderlands. Roerich's predicament as a painter reveals the Inner Asian complexities of the early twentieth century. But cultural enthusiasts have referred to Roerich not as a bystander who appreciated the beauty of the Altai but as one who was spiritually motivated by the legend of White Tsar that bonded people from various hues and backgrounds. Both Roerich and Sankrityayana, despite the difference in their approaches, wrote about the cosmopolitan traits of Asiatic borderlands of Soviet Russia. Both reflected on the span and scale of human phenomena in Russia's southern and eastern borderlands. In Roerich's writings, Altai is revealed as a cultural landscape. Sankrityayana on the other hand presents the socialist reality of Siberia's Mongolian borderlands. The writings are merited as cultural treatises—Roerich's account has striking relevance in the realm of 'spiritual geopolitics'[23] and Sankrityayana's autobiography is a rich source material on the socialist euphoria.

For the second essay, I have concentrated on selected writings of Chokan Valikhanov that were republished in IRGO annals and were translated later by those in service of the British imperial service.[24] The primary objective for this was to understand Valikhanov's pioneering role as the Kazakh ambassador who inspired his fellow people to follow a tradition of learning. Some of Valikhanov's ideas on Kazakh enlightenment were quoted in Soviet history annals. Moreover, Valikhanov like Abay Kunanbaev was projected as an ideological icon by the celebrated Kazakh writer Mukhtar Auezov. Auezov's trilogy *Abay Zholy*, a fictionalized work on the life of Abay is indicative of the nineteenth-century Kazakh intellectual milieu that was influenced by Russian folklore, music and every other form of popular Russian culture. Kermit E. McKenzie's English-language biography on Valikhanov is a useful source on Valikhanov's mission as Kazakh envoy. It also is an impressive account of his career graph that proved his credentials as an ethnographer and military geographer.[25] Valikhanov transmitted every piece of local information that guided not only his imperial masters but also his fellow Kazakhs. Interpretative analysis on the subject of Kazakh intellectualism is a revelation of the Kazakh social milieu of the nineteenth and twentieth centuries. The works of Sabol and Tomohiko on the role of the Kazakh newspaper *Dala Walayatining Gazeti* to create an interactive space—an initiative that was sponsored by the imperial administration constitute an important segment of my second essay that deals with Kazakh conscience.

For the third essay that is primarily focused on the idealism of Siberian *oblastnichestvo*, N.M. Yadrintsev's treatise *Sibir' kak koloniya* has been treated at length. The section that has been specially consulted is the *oblastniki's* views on the *inorodetsy* (aliens). The interpretation of Yadrintsev's works by Siberian historians like L.M. Goryushkin, M.V. Shilovsky and Natalia Ablazhei indicate the impact of *oblastnichestvo* on the Siberian psyche.[26] The content-analysis of the *oblastniki* newspaper *Vostochnoe Obozrenie* by Maria Eva Stolberg has special value. The interdisciplinary journal *Sibirica* reflects a different interest in *oblastnichestvo*. Some of the analytical articles in the journals have examined the socio-cultural ideals of the movement that were not restricted to the Russian circuit but had a wider coverage. The purpose of *Sibirica* is to make its readers aware of Siberia's Asia connection. The report on Yadrintsev's travel missions to the Mongolian border is one such indication.[27] An implication of this survey mission was to establish bonding with the Buryat-Mongol counterparts of the *oblastniki*.

For a general overview of Soviet studies on Siberia and Kazakhstan, I consulted special issues of *Voprosy Istorii* and *Istoriya SSSR* of the 1950s and the 1960s. Most of these volumes were 'anniversary issues' and were devoted to the role of the Communist Party in bringing about development and progress in the region. A large amount of this historical literature, including the multi-volume history of Siberia (*Istoriya Sibiri*), encyclopaedias and directories (*Russki Biograficheski Slovar*), and books on Kazakh people or Siberian cities pop out from the dusty shelves of the National Library's Russian section.[28] The Gorky Sadan Library, despite its decaying collection, is a surprise because of the good amount of Auezov's works that are available there. It should be mentioned here that this library has a good collection of the works of Sadridin Aini, the Tajik intellectual as well as that of Chingiz Aitmatov, the Kyrgyz writer.

My impressions of post-Soviet research trends are guided by the literary works of regional historians on historical subjects. The gift literature of Novosibirsk's Institute of History, Irkutsk's Inner Asia research wing and Kazakhstan's Institute of Oriental Studies, is of great value. The observations that have been made by experts during interactive meets also convey a message—there needs to be a perceptive analysis and not a guided approach to the study of the region. Writings pertaining to culture often tend to criticize the streamlining of disciplines.[29] Max Planck Institute of Social Anthropology has a vibrant study group, Siberian Studies Centre. The Centre's specialists, especially Joachim Otto Habeck and his team who work on the Far North, are deeply interested in creating an ambience for interdisciplinary methodologies that could be extremely relevant for the study of Eurasia's borderland cultures. Web journals like *Ab Imperio, Acta Slavica Iaponica, Sibirskaia Zaimka* have also been consulted for the period 2002-8. Writings in these journals indicate the broad reach of episodic moments in steppe history—ranging from nineteenth-century governance in Omsk to twentieth-century cataclysmic events like the famine on Kazakh land structure[30] and the impact of Allied intervention on the revolutionary strongholds in Siberia.[31] Of paramount importance is the JSTOR archives (a digital archive of leading social science journals) which has a huge chunk of materials on the 'opening up of Siberia' by Russia. Sometimes, the review literature that was published in some of these journals has also been of great help in understanding trends of research. Novosibirsk's *Gumanytarnye Nauki v Sibiri* also has its own agenda for regional studies.

On the whole, in attempting to draw out specific historiographical patterns that complement or contest each other, the study attempts to specify the steppe as an important category. This categorization seems to have been lacking in Soviet writings though the authorities were extremely sensitive to regime-controlled border issues. Due to post-Soviet revelations, such categories have seen the light of the day.

NOTES

1. Sir Arnold Joseph Toynbee, *A Study of History* (12 vols.), London: Oxford University Press, 1940; John F. Baddley, *The Ragged Flanks of the Caucasus* (2 vols.), London: Oxford University Press, 1940; John F. Baddley, *The Russian Conquest of the Caucasus*, London: Longmans, Green, 1940; Dominic Lieven, *Empire: The Russian Empire and its Rivals*, London: John Murray, 2000; Rene Grousset, *The Empire of the Steppes: A History of Central Asia* (originally published in French in 1939 and republished in five English editions till 1997).
2. G.M. Hamburg, 'Imperial Entanglements: Two New Histories of Russia's Western and Southern Borderlands', *Kritika: Explorations in Russian and Eurasian History*, 9, 2, Spring 2008 [book review of Robert D. Crews, *For Prophet and Tsar: Islam and Empire in Russia and Central Asia*, Cambridge, M.A.: Harvard University Press, 2006 and Mikhail Dmitrievich Dolbilov and Aleksei Il'ich Miller, *Zapadnye okrainy Rossiskoi imperii*, Moscow: Novoe Literaturnoe Obozrenie, 2006].
3. *Entsiklopediceskii*, *Slovar*, Leipzig: Brockhauz and Efron, 1890-1917, MFS 6978 and MFS 6979 in National Library, Kolkata.
4. In 1914, there were eleven Cossack 'hosts' strung out from river Don in the west to the rivers Amur and Ussuri in the Far East.
5. James H. Bater and R.A French (eds.), *Studies in Russian Historical Geography*, London: Academic Press, 1983. Specially the chapters 'Approaches to the Historical Geography of Russia' and 'The Frontier in Central Asia'.
6. The territory of the Tungus people is very large, extending beyond the Lena and Lake Baikal. The Tungus territory belongs to two ethnic groups—the Turkic Yakuts and the Mongol Buryats. It is this shared

space between the Buryats and the Tungus in the Lake Baikal region that can be roughly treated as the grass steppe of Asiatic Russia.

7. James Forsyth, *A History of the Peoples of Siberia: Russia's North Asian Colony, 1581-1990*, Cambridge: Cambridge University Press, 1992.
8. M. Viatkin, *Ocherki po istorii Kazakhskoi SSSR do drevneishykh vremen po 1870 gody*, Tom pervyi, Ogiz Gospolitizdat, 1941.
9. James Forsyth, *A History of the Peoples of Siberia: Russia's North Asian Colony 1581-1990*, Cambridge: Cambridge University Press, 1992.
10. The Mongol phenomenon in steppe history is a revelation. A limited group of scholars including Nicholas Cosmo, Stephen Kotkin, Reuven Amitai and Michal Biran have taken the initiative of projecting steppe history through Mongol lens.
11. Arup Banerji, *Making the Past Work: Writing History in the Soviet Union*, New Delhi: Social Science Press, 2008, introductory chapter.
12. Anatole G. Mazour, *Modern Russian Historiography* (rev. edn.), Westport, Connecticut: Greenwood Press, 1975; Mazour, *The Writing of History in the Soviet Union*, Stanford: Hoover Institution Press, 1971.
13. Anatole G. Mazour, *The Writing of History in the Soviet Union*, introduction and first chapter that discuss in detail the character of 'disciplining' of historical writing.
14. Tragic episodes of heroism or accounts of bravery were published by the most popular publishing house of Moscow, Progress Publishers. There is one such narration of Soviet rescuers trying to rescue the diary of a Soviet railway engineer and surveyor who perished in the Kazyr rapids in the Sayan mountains in 1942. Vladimir Chivilikhin, *Wilderness Survey: True Story of a Taiga Tragedy*, Moscow: Progress Publishers (date of publication not printed in the book).
15. On Magnitogorsk, see Stephen Kotkin, *Magnetic Mountain: Stalinism as a Civilization*, Berkeley: University of California Press, 1995; Stephen Kotkin, *Steel Town*, Berkeley: University of California Press; John Scott, *Behind the Urals: An American Worker in Russia's City of Steel*, Bloomington: Indiana University Press, 1942. Enlarged edition prepared by Stephen Kotkin, 1989. On Vladivostok, see William Richardson (University of Washington, Tacoma), 'Bolshoi Vladivostok: Architecture and Urban Planning in the Stalinist Era' (William Richardson, 'Bolshoi Vladivostak....' Depts.washington.edu/reecas/events/conf2002/papers02/Richardson.doc). On Soviet planning, see Fiona Hill and Clifford Gaddy, *The Siberian Curse: How Communist Planners Left Russia Out in the Cold*, Brookings Institution Press, 2003, pp. 70-1.
16. Nick Baron, 'New Spatial Histories of 20th Century Russia and the Soviet Union: Exploring the Terrain' (review article), *Kritika: Explorations in Russian and Eurasian History,* 9, 2, Spring 2008, p. 433.

17. Despite acknowledgement of Soviet academic pursuits regarding a land-man environment, the British scholars felt that there was hardly any attempt to establish an independent line of argument. Criticizing Soviet studies of the 1960s and the 1970s, R.A. French and James Bater argued that there was no worthwhile progress in the realm of historical geography as far as the Soviet Union was concerned because the academicians always felt the pressure of party-oriented or policy-oriented research. The style of Soviet historical writing hardly offered anything new in content or method and little awareness about spatial concepts. James H. Bater and R.A. French (eds.), *Studies in Russian Historical Geography*, vol. I, London: Academic Press, 1983, p. 4.
18. Rahul Sankrityayana, *Meri Jeevan Yatra* (tr. into Bengali as *Amar Jibon Jatra*), ed. Satish Mitra and Saikat Rakshit, Rahul Sankrityayana Birth Centenary Committee, 5 vols. Kolkata, 1995.
19. Owen Lattimore, *Inner Asian Frontiers of China*, Hong Kong: Oxford University Press, 1988 (republished); Owen Lattimore, *Studies in Frontier History: Collected Papers, 1928-1958*, London: Oxford University Press, 1962.
20. M. Viatkin, *Ocherki po istorii Kazakhskoi SSSR do drevneishykh vremen po 1870 gody*, Tom pervyi, Ogiz Gospolitizdat, 1941.
21. L.M. Goryushkin, 'Glavniy trud N.M. Yadrintseva' in *Sibir' kak koloniya v geograficheskom, etnograficheskom I istoricheskom otnoshenii,* of the series *Istoriya istochniki: pervoistochniki*, Vypusk III, Novosibirsk, 2003.
22. Sankrityayana, op. cit. Nicholas Roerich, *Heart of Asia*, Varanasi: Pilgrims Publishing, 2007; Roerich, *Altai-Himalaya (A Travel Diary)*, Delhi: Book Faith India, 1929 (republished in 1996).
23. John McCannon, 'By the Shores of White Waters: The Altai and its Place in the Spiritual Geopolitics of Nicholas Roerich', *Sibirica*, vol. 2, no. 2, October 2002.
24. Captain Valikanof, M. Veniukof and other Russian travellers, *The Russians in Central Asia: Their Occupation of the Kyrgyz Steppe and the Line of the Syr Darya: Their Political Relations with Khiva, Bokhara and Kokan, also Descriptions of Chinese Turkestan and Dzhungaria* (tr. from the Russian by John and Robert Michell), London: Edward Stanford, 1865.
25. Kermit E. McKenzie, 'Chokan Valikhanov: Kazakh Princeling and Scholar', *Central Asian Survey*, 8 (3), 1989.
26. N.N. Ablazhei, *Sibirs'koe oblastnichestvo v emigratsii,* Novosibirsk: Institute of Archaeology and Ethnography RAN, 2003; Shilovky's article in http://oblastnichestvo.lib.tomsk.ru/page.php?id=2
27. H.S. Hundley, 'N.M. Yadrintsev and the search for Ghengis Khan's Capital, Kharakorum' [research report], *Sibirica,* vol. 7, issue 2, Autumn 2008.

28. An example is N. Yanovskii, *Pisateli Sibirii (izbrannie stati)*, Moscow: Sovremennik, 1988.
29. There have been pointed observations about the redundant nature of ethnographic methodologies. Patty Gray, Nikolai Vakhtin and Peter Schweitzer, 'Who Owns Siberian Ethnography? A Critical Assessment of a Re-internationalized Field', *Sibirica*, vol. 3, no. 2, October 2003.
30. An example—Niccolo Pianciola, 'Famine in the Steppe: The Collectivization of Agriculture and Kazak Herdsmen', *Cahiers du Monde Russe,* 45/1-2, Janvier-June 2004.
31. An example—'Belaia Sibir', special issue in electronic journal *Sibirskaia Zaimka*, vol. 7, 2007.

CHAPTER 1

The Steppe as Frontier

FRONTIER STUDIES REVISITED

In the post-disintegration period, there seems to have been a qualitative leap in portrayals of Eurasian history—frontiers and borderlands are idealized as interactive spaces and are no longer ignored as peripheral in terms of the universe of control. In recent borderland studies of the Eurasian region, the focus is not only on the dominant constellations of the Russian empire but also on the local dynamics of Russia's southern, western and eastern borderlands.[1] So discussions about imperial Russia's borderlands are not only limited to heartland debates and the intricacies of colonial apparatus but also include local histories and interplay of local forces. Scholars began to address the issue of how frontiers reciprocated, communicated or collaborated in what was considered to be a diehard imperial set up. There seems to have been a greater interest in borderland communities not so much as organized polities within the larger institutional state structure, but as locomotives for economic growth and centres for innovation and we are reminded of the space of the Eurasian frontier—connoting not only territorial but also economic, social, religious, intellectual—and the determination of the interrelationships between human beings. So, it is human sciences and its subject 'man' that has acquired a prominent position in Eurasian history. Besides the human phenomena it is also the natural processes, i.e. mountains, river basins, nature reserves that integrate settlement areas. The rapidly expanding interdisciplinary field about borderlands and frontiers therefore tends to resurrect the image of the frontier as a human setting. The Eurasian frontier, the stereotypical other in a colonized setting, is reappraised as a human environment.

The idea of a frontier as a human space is not new—its implication as a special category and an extent of human settlement and a demographic pattern as well as living conditions *along a specific frontier line* is almost a century and a half old. Since Frederick Jackson Turner's 1893 thesis about frontiers as moving spaces that were linked to America's development, there have been a multitude of interpretations about imperial frontiers, eastern and western frontiers. The Wisconsin historian Frederick Jackson Turner broached this subject in 1893 by saying that there has been a continually advancing American frontier in the westward direction. This aspect of human mobility is the Turnerian explanation of the fluidity of American life and social development. Turner regarded America's development as progressive colonization which had a positive effect. 'Moving westward, the frontier became more and more American', emphasized Turner. Turner's point was that America's frontier of settlement had changed significantly and isolated settlements had left the frontier line undefined.[2] He expressed his feelings about 'vital forces' in American society that turned the scales in favour of development. This view of frontiers, mostly related to the American experience, has been critically examined and scholars till date have expressed divergent views about 'societies in motion'. Turner's critics disapproved of his concept of 'a forward movement' towards the frontier, arguing that a frontier in the Turnerian sense is *imagined* as progressive. There are counter-arguments too and advocates of geopolitics who regard the frontier as a power grid have supported Turner's view as pragmatic and his prognosis about 'progression' as very down-to-earth.

Irrespective of their methodological differences, there is consensus among the Turner and anti-Turner camps about the frontier as a determinant of history with various sub-types: (a) state-managed boundaries set by military conquest, (b) ethnic divisions, (c) physiographical and geographical units, (d) human spaces having linguistic and social contexts. The emphasis has shifted from the first to the last, i.e. from conquest and resistance to cultural interaction, interrogation of geographical visions, multiple loci and images of frontier utopias.[3]

In contemporary frontier discourse too, attention is focused on the multitude of interpretations about the usage of the term 'frontier' in the Turnerian sense. A comparative viewpoint has taken the debate to a different level.[4] It is not only Turner's methodological assumptions that are discussed but also intellectual and ideological trends that influenced him, namely *anthropogeographie* or human geography, environmentalism and other natural science disciplines.[5] The second aspect is the recognition of the 'frontier' as a social space, taking into account human elements (e.g. nomads, pilgrims, traders, émigrés) redefined as communities in motion and belonging to a contact zone and not to a controlled military space or a delimited terrain. So, 'frontier' is a changing concept and is, in contemporary academic discourse, linked to a global process of human interaction. In this particular category are Siberian historians who influenced by the theoretical premises of Turner's model, apply them to their own postulates about Siberia's interactive frontiers.[6] Siberia's historians are indebted to Turner for his suggestions about frontier dynamism. They share his conviction that frontier contacts and spontaneous movement of people in the frontiers impacted on imperial institutions. Their subject of analysis is frontiers not as the outer domain of an expansionist empire but as provinces and regions with experiences of development and contact with metropolitan centres like Moscow and St. Petersburg. In the words of M.V. Shilovsky, the interactive process of Russia's frontiers in Siberia spanned over four centuries during which the Tsarist state through its able military officers and administrators *formed* its frontier through a coercive-cum-organizational mechanism (exile, deportation, banishment as well as settlement). Shilovsky gauged the Siberian frontier in terms of its demographic character and migratory processes.[7] By idealizing the history of their provinces, Siberia's historians have added a new dimension to the format of frontier studies. Their interests seem to converge with the field interest of the practitioners of other disciplines, namely social anthropology.

Turner's American hypothesis is compared with the Asian perspective of another pioneer of frontier history, Owen Lattimore (1900-89)[8] and his influential paradigm of 'China's marginal territories'.[9] The methods of Lattimore's analysis are applied to a vast range of spatial arenas: to the borderlands of China, to Japan, to Europe and America and to the world as a whole.[10] Frontier studies gathered momentum with Owen Lattimore's dictum of Inner Asian frontiers of China that converged or overlapped with Mongolian and Russian frontiers. Frontier-related questions have stressed on the potency of Lattimore's hypothesis about the adaptability of Chinese frontiers. Lattimore's *Asia Lecture* at the Royal Geographical Society in 1928 about caravan routes in Inner Asia was based on his ground observations about land routes in Chinese Turkestan.[11] The lecture pointed to the adaptability of nomadic traders to the uses of civilized trade and raised questions about a very current debate, i.e. migration. What fascinated Lattimore, who called himself an 'unscientific geographer', was that the caravan traders were migrants who in the 1920s were continually moving to and from Inner and Outer Mongolia, which were the spheres of Chinese and Russian influence, respectively and were continually adjusting themselves to new situations in order to avert the dangers of border transgression. Related subjects (the reservoir of frontiers, comparative frontiers, and so on) were addressed further by Lattimore in his 'serial publications' in *Atlantic Monthly* (1934), *The Geographical Review* (1937), *The Journal of Economic History* (1947) and *The Geographical Journal* (1953) as well as in the form of several book chapters that were republished by some of these as well as other journals (e.g. *Pacific Affairs*).[12] Lattimore's arguments about fluctuating relationships between Central Asian nomads and Chinese sedentary population challenged the fixity of historical analysis. His ideas about 'a recognizable periodicity in the fluctuations of steppe history'[13] and his perspectives about a correlation between Chinese imperial history and steppe identity, illustrated by Chinese border influences on nomadic steppe economy of Mongolia, Manchuria and Tibet were revelations of Eurasian frontier history. Scholars belonging to the Lattimorian tradition refer to their mentor's model about frontier zones and reiterate his stance about the interaction of society and environment in the Inner Asian frontiers of China,[14] the tribal frontiers of Iran, religious frontiers of the Ottomans, and so on. Lattimore's followers have reviewed the ideological trend and the entire corpus of literature about human geography that guided their master.[15]

The purpose of contemporary discourse is not simply a recovery of the Turnerian and Lattimorian models. Contemporary analysts, influenced by their mentors, have also stressed the relevance of the frontier as a useful tool of historical analysis and the focus is on the timelessness of the Eurasian frontier. The analysis shifts from military frontiers as a defence mechanism, i.e. a fort chain managed by Russian generals during the fifteenth to the eighteenth centuries to a pre-Tsarist setting of military regimes and art of war of the Turko-Mongol warriors in the steppe (Inner Asia, Central Asia and Siberia), the instrumentality of imperial culture, and so on. Other parameters have been added—human relationships and exchange patterns integral to the steppe ecosystem. Such divergent analyses reflect the ongoing debate about frontiers, largely focusing on the steppe territory that overlaps with Chinese, Russian, Mongol and Central Asian territories. The focus is also on a long tradition of frontier historiography that assesses a series of interrelated phenomena about dynastic change, tribal confederacies, imperial takeovers, frontier alignments and regional sentiments. Spokesman of frontier historiography in Russia, Asia and the West, irrespective of whether they preach or reject the Turnerian and Lattimorian variants, have referred to such interrelated episodes in history.[16] In the upcoming sections, we will study the paradigm flows and the diversions in approach and the dissemination of ideas of Turner and Lattimore by successive generations. There are a number of 'voices', each representing a methodological approach which is unique in its own way. There is a Russia-dominated monochromatic view as well as polycentric views represented by a host of others. While the general approach is to raise questions within an imperial framework, specific instances have been cited to explain what the frontier disposition was all about. So, besides a Russia-centric image, there are ideas about a Mongol *mysl,* a Chinese hangover, Siberian *oblastnichestvo* as an intellectual awakening and Alash Orda political activism reinforced by a Kazakh 'conscience'. The frontier character is also revealed by the profile of Cossackdom, representing the Cossacks as a military category, i.e. a Russian service community providing military back-up to the Muscovite princes. There are also other aspects as Cossack group behaviour and camouflaging instincts, daunting tactics and rebelliousness of Pugachev and Stepan Razin, that have erased dark memories of Cossacks as savage mounted horsemen of the White Army during the period of the Civil War.[17] The aspect of Muslim spirituality and Muslim institutional legacies in Kazakh urban settings is also a subject of new-age literature,[18] otherwise left unattended in a maze of steppe identities essentially confined to pastoral activities of nomads or clan lineages. The transcendental awareness about Muslim steppe believers and pre-Islamic religious faith among the Inner Asians[19] add new dimension to the gamut of steppe studies.

Rene Grousset: Long Duree Steppe History

Frontier hypotheses have unfolded narratives about nomad history and nomad domain. The earliest among them is Rene Grousset's *The Empire of the Steppes: A History of Central Asia* (originally published in French in 1939 and translated into

English by Naomi Walford after the French edition of 1952 and was republished in 1970 and 1997) that traces the forceful entry into Asia by Hunnic tribes, Mongol marauders and Golden Horde nomads and the pressures of their movements eastward and westward that largely affected China, Persia, India and Europe. Grousset's account elaborates dynastic history of nomadic regimes, personified by mighty men like Attila, Chingiz Khan and Timur Lane. It is also a repertoire of impressions about a human habitat (represented by a combination of pastoral farmers, herders and hunters) that was hurled into the midst of internal competition among Turko-Mongol tribes and that had numberless tracks that subsequently became 'the route of barbarism' by the warrior-leaders mentioned above. The motivation of the expeditions was pastures and the desire to find new grazing lands. What followed were alignments with the sedentary people that never lasted long—a line of thought that was contested later—because it was in the nomads' character to raid and rule. What ought to be remembered however, in Grousset-style, is the governance of leaders that was largely based on an exchange system. Leadership control was an asset as far as the nomads were concerned and according to Grousset, would possibly rescue them from obscurity.

Grousset's tone is not flattering though he begins by describing the bounties of the steppe in antiquity. The interactive space denoted that stretch of territory that was inhabited by the trans-Asian nomadic tribes and the various Eurasian routes that they traversed. Their routes originated in the steppe belt stretching between the Caucasus and the Black Sea coast, the Urals and up to Siberia's Minusinsk basin—a fairly large stretch with a pronounced exchange of art forms which indicate how Iranian, Indo-European groups (Greek and Scythian) coalesced. Relics indicate that the western part of the steppe zone was occupied by the nomads of the Iranian stock while the southern and eastern parts were under the sway of the Turko-Mongol people. Subsequently, it was a nation of nomad governors and army commanders, belonging to the Hunnic hierarchy who dominated the steppe's eastern part, especially the Transbaikal region, 'outer' Mongolia and some Chinese outposts close to the Tarim Basin. It was this Hunnic group that was engaged in a tussle for control over the kingdom of Turfan and the Tarim oases after the decline of the Han dynasty. The ascendancy of this group was combated by semi-independent Chinese principalities of Yarkand and Khotan who with the support of some Indo-European tribal groups like the Scythians, Sogdians and the Yeuh Chih wanted to remove their competitors from the historic silk route zone. The southern silk route passing through Yarkand and Khotan became a busy trade route and an important route of exchange between Buddhist missionaries, monks, translators and art dealers. Grousset's monumental work surveys ten centuries of steppe history, highlighting every phase of nomadic control, dissemination of that control in the form of Turkic dominions in Transoxiana, Mongol tutelage of Chingiz Khan, the nomadic sojourns of Chingiz Khan's descendant Batu. The attempt to 'reorient' the Mongol khanate in the thirteenth century and the resuscitation of Turkic power were other aspects of an internal revival. According to Grousset, the Turkic takeover lacked resonance compared to the scale of Chingizid control. Chingiz Khan's rule was legitimized by the sanction of law. So, the Chingiz Khanite legacy was law-governed and accounted for the survival of a regime which in no way 'dissolved' or 'disintegrated' after the thirteenth century.

Grousset's long duree approach about steppe history was also adopted by Denis Sinor, the Hungarian Sinologist who viewed the region as Inner Asia that evolved as a zone of perpetual conflict between the encircling sedentary population and the Inner Asian people. Sinor's premise was that the sedentary people made inroads (mainly retaliatory attacks) from the periphery towards the heartland which expanded the size of Inner Asia. There were periodic contractions and expansions, which depended largely on the level of interactions between the Inner Asians and the regions around them. Sinor and his team pointed out that it was the steppe's self-sufficient methods (animal husbandry, cattle breeding) that kept them isolated from the agriculturists. The nomads were able to sustain themselves but also complemented their production with commodities from outside, especially from agricultural regions. They adopted an exchange method only when necessary. So, the root of difference lay in the economic factors which caused a confrontational relationship between the two sides.[20] Reuven Amitai and Michael Biran on the other hand were more keen to indicate interaction between the two sides and highlighted the role of Eurasia's steppe nomads in the affairs of the sedentary people of the neighbouring countries. The writers speak of a large chronological span—about three millennia from 1100 BC to Eurasian pastoral nomadism today and highlights the 500 year history (tenth to fifteenth centuries) as the age of the nomads. From ancient times through the middle ages and into the modern period, the intriguing element is the level and scale of operation of the pastoral nomads, how they mingled with their sedentary neighbours, their complex contacts and exchanges that varied from synthesis to open conflict. The turning point in steppe history, they argue, is the Mongols' land empire, that needs to be reckoned as a 'world empire' because of the large swath of the world stretching from East Asia to eastern Europe and the Mediterranean and thousands of years of contacts and confrontation that took place within this space. The Mongol phenomenon is also part of world history because the nomads conveyed ideas and also transported merchandise, technology and cultural artefacts from one end of Eurasia to another.[21] These and other specifics of the Mongol interlude have led David Morgan and Stephen Kotkin to certify it as a fascinating period of Eurasian history. These specifics are (a) the Mongols' law code or the order of the *yasa* that was permanently binding on the subjects and their descendants and (b) the Mongol cosmos that had a unique pattern of governance. Morgan elaborates on the *yasa* as an elaborate imperial institution[22] while Kotkin describes the strategy of governance of the Mongols. Kotkin argues about the Mongol commonwealth, referring to the matrix of identities that arose out of an exchange pattern between the Mongols, Turkic groups and the Tatars. The Mongol commonwealth to Kotkin represents a cosmos that links all the stars. In his re-examination of the nomadic paradigm, Kotkin makes passionate claims about Mongol imperial culture. He expresses staunch ideas about the empire of Chingiz Khan and the Mongol *ulus* and the Mongols' superb mastery in the realm of exchange and governance.[23] In Kotkin's analysis, such empires fade from memory because of the heightened attention to borderlands.[24]

The new genre of writings has thus pinpointed the following: a series of historical phenomena, a Eurasian spectrum of political upheavals and migratory movements of nomadic tribes, the expansion and contraction of nomadic confederations that impacted not only on the nomadic economy (pastoralism),[25] but also on interrelations between nomads and their sedentary neighbours (e.g. the Uighurs of China) and between subsets of the two nomadic groups, the Mongols and the Turks. The framework of nomadic studies extends to a range of ideas about integration instead of disintegration, cohesion instead of diffusion, continuities instead of discontinuities. Scholars have critiqued generalizations and assumptions about disintegration of the nomadic empire in the late thirteenth century. The stereotypes of a nomadic domain have been challenged and the 'trade or raid' motives of the nomads have been scrutinized. Also, the ways in which the nomads 'secured' their relationships with their sedentary neighbours have been taken into consideration.[26]

'Ab Imperio' et al.: The Russian Frontier Setting

Writings in the Kazan-based journal *Ab Imperio* have focused on the lacunae in the dominant paradigm about frontier discourse and have provided alternative arguments about frontier alignments. In almost every issue of *Ab Imperio* that has been published since 2000, historians, archivists and social anthropologists have expressed new ideas about borderlands, criticized stereotypes of representation, questioned premises of dominant narratives (colonial or nationalist) that have ignored borderland issues or have downplayed local sentiments and have debated on whether there should be a reordering of disciplines like history, social anthropology and political geography. In *Ab Imperio's* special issue (no. 1, 2003), the authors have analysed the multiplicity of approaches, the dialectics and ambiguities of post-colonial perspectives, severely criticizing the methodology which did not take into account the questions of identity and history of the frontier and borderland. According to *Ab Imperio's* editorial board, because of the variety of experiences, every perspective about Eurasia needs to be compared and reviewed. The essays pertain to social collectivities and group performances that were left unspecified previously. The general presumption of this section of writers is that meta-narratives about the empire do not sufficiently address the issue of the frontier. Hence, the idea of the special volume was 'to allow the frontier cross its limits' and emerge from its marginalized status as a research theme and set an agenda for borderlands that could evolve as a mediating narrative.[27] It is worth examining few of the *Ab Imperio's* articles that enquire about uncharted terrains of Russian imperial history.

A principal area of investigation is historiography and historiographical traditions. Alfred Rieber's survey of nineteenth-century frontier historiography is a sophisticated treatment of changing concepts. It indicates how the frontier has changed its format—from a linear and spatial concept to a *process* with geographical, historical and cultural attributes. Rieber moves from the mainframe of Turner's thesis to several comparative approaches that experimented with numerous ideas as 'symbolic geographies', 'linguistic representations', and so on. Symbolism became a major preoccupation for scholars who followed Frederik Barth's paradigm of symbolic boundary and writers like Tatyana Skrynnikova and Sergei Abashin proclaimed their versions of symbolic frontiers as integral components of the frontier metanarrative.[28] Elena

Bezvikonnaia repositioned the Omsk region as a special category in Russian imperial state-building of the 1820s and the 1830s.[29] Other methodologies and trajectories also came to the forefront as disciplines like anthropology, history and geography interacted with each other to explore the possibilities of 'communication' in the Slavic world through say, language and linguistic affinities. The linguistic category was addressed by Suzanne Wertheim in her analysis of 'linguistic performance' by the Tatars,[30] David Laitin in his analysis of the dynamism of shared languages that practically bonded linguistic communities across linguistic boundaries.[31] These articles, as those of other contributors in the volume, have viewed Eurasia's frontiers as interactive and communicative, adding thereby a major boost to 'the view from the margins'. There is therefore a complete role reversal as far as Eurasia's frontiers are concerned and both Alfred Rieber and Andreas Kappeler tend to take this point further in their overall appreciation about overlapping frontiers. Having mentioned four main categories of Eurasia's frontier (geographical frontier, social frontier, military frontier and cultural frontier), Kappeler argues that it is the frontier mentality that is the crucial issue that has shaped the contours of relationship between the Muscovite state on the one hand and the Cossacks, steppe nomads (the Kazakhs and the Naimans and also the Kalmyks), forest groups in the Urals and the Finno-Ugric ethnic stock and the indigenous people of northern Siberia on the other.[32] Kappeler was inspired by the individual roles that frontiers played as a competitive as well as an integrative force. Referring to clan ties of Russia's southern and eastern borderlands (comprising Kazakhs, Kalmyks and Tatars of the Golden Horde or the Nogai tribe), Kappeler argues that the steppe frontier of Russia evolved since the sixteenth century from an 'extractive frontier' in western Siberia close to the Urals (where exploitation took place) to a 'settlement frontier' beyond the Urals and south Siberia (where Kazakhs entered Russian military service). In Kappeler's hypothesis, the military frontier of Russia was very distinct from the social frontier that the Cossacks represented.

The military frontier was hardly progressive in the Turnerian sense, argues Kappeler, because of the dual mechanism of conflict and communication. Tsarist Russia's conflictual relationship with steppe inhabitants was an integral and dominant feature of steppe memory. At the same time, there was intensive commercial and diplomatic exchange, i.e. the 'partner exchanges' between Moscow on the one hand and various Tatar groups (e.g. Nogai princes, Kazakh sultans) on the other. So, Kappeler has a double judgement about Russia's frontiers: (a) as combative and resistant and (b) as complementary and communicative. Speaking of Moscow's relationship of conflict with frontier groups, Kappeler refers to Siberia's 'extractive and settlement frontiers' represented by forest communities (fur gatherers and metal processors). The Kazakhs and the Tatars were the communicative groups while the Cossacks were the dynamic group with a social status in the imperial setup.

Kappeler's differential analysis of the frontier is an indication of the variations in interpretations that exist among regional historians and how these were interwoven as expressions of an overall steppe identity. According to Kappeler, the frontier has evolved as a historian's choice and is represented differently in different periods.[33]

The Turbulent Mind: Michael Khodarkovsky

In Michael Khodarkovsky, we hardly find such timid acceptance of a submissive frontier mentality. Khodarkovsky is outspoken about ground reality and is straightforward in his views about Russia's restive frontier which made 'peace impossible'.[34] Khodarkovsky views the frontier as a zone of imperial encounter and points out Russia's contestations with her southern borderlands. Khodarkovsky differs from the corpus of literature that focuses on Russia's military fortifications, construction of forts and fort-towns, military outposts (*voevodas*), the settlement of pioneers and peasant settlers and the role of the Cossack regiment. His narrative is an exception not because it touches upon the unequal political relationship between the ruler and the ruled, but because it conveys the depth of Russia's steppe relations and explains the contours of an ambiguous relationship. Khodarkovsky is very categorical about the underlying difference: the steppe in the post-Mongoloid phase represents a confederation of tribes none of which shared any kind of political affinity. Each of them was economically self-sufficient and politically independent and hence one couldn't expect a tie-up among such loose fragmented units. What Grousset referred to was the twelfth-century grand political order of the Chingizid *yasa* which held the unit together. What Khodarkovsky was referring to was the post-Chingizid break-up—the scattered remnants of control among the Nogais, the Kalmyks and the Kazakhs. These tribal units were extremely disunited and could not unite under a common legacy, corresponding either to the Mongol khanate or to the Golden Horde. The ruling dynasties of the Kazakhs and the Nogais tried to survive through strategies like alliance-building with the non-Chingizid nobility and dispense with the danger of a house divided over the issue of control over pasturelands or the collection of taxes. Khodarkovsky is caustic in his remarks about the tricky situations encountered by the Russians. The Turko-Mongol hybrid mix represented diverse interests and it was practically impossible for the Russians to control these groups reliant on immediate gains through war and raid.

An added worry was the plight of Russian slaves: held in captivity in the courts of Nogai or Crimean Khans, these slaves were freed by their captors as exchange items of a deal that amounted to the payment of a huge ransom by the Russian government. Very often the deals failed to the detriment and misery of the slaves.[35] Not only could the Russians not control the Nogais and fulfil their conditions about Russian slaves, but also failed to assert themselves when the Nogais laid claims on the horse trade that flourished on the Crimean coast. What the Russians could do in the fifteenth century was to look for alternative routes of trade along which they could trade amidst far better conditions with the Indian, Persian, Bukharan merchants than the Nogais. The situation was slightly more difficult in the sixteenth century when the Kalmyks, a community of Buddhists, penetrated the Astrakhan region, moving from Inner Asia towards the Caspian Sea and pushing towards the Russian strongholds in Kazan and Ufa districts. The Kalmyks were unrelenting and did not succumb to the Russians. In fact, they insulted the Russian envoys on several occasions and declined to take oaths of allegiance. It was not before the eighteenth century when the Kalmyks' herds started decreasing that they began their exodus towards Dzhungaria. The remnants of the Kalmyk Chancellery were entrusted in the hands of a Russian supervisor (*glavnyi pristav*) and with that was handled the Kalmyk impasse.

In the eighteenth century, the Russians had lesser trouble with the Kazakh sultans who had already in the sixteenth century entered into some kind of an alliance by rendering protection to the Russian trading caravans coming from the direction of Orenburg. The strategic alliance secured the Russians and tamed their Nogai and Oirat competitors in the trading business. In the eighteenth century, the imperial rulers achieved the fruits of these alliances—the Kazakh sultans were allowed to police the Orenburg region acquired by the Russians. The negotiations that followed (e.g. Russians allowing Kazakhs to loot caravans plying the territory) indicated that both sides theoretically were committed to maintaining a relationship of tolerance though the reality seemed to be quite different. The Russians, for example, were unable to accommodate sultan Abul Khair's claims about a military fortress on the Syr Darya or support him militarily in his siege over Khiva.[36] Subsequently, some of Orenburg's governors connived with the rival clans of Abul Khair with the hope that the Khan would be more amenable to Russian mercantilist interests. But Abul Khair's successors were as evasive as their predecessor and the Russian predicament of controlling Kazakh chieftains on the border of the Yaik River was to continue till the nineteenth century. According to Khodarkovsky, therefore, there was no denying of the fact that Russia's expanded steppe dominions in the west and the south faced tough competition from the Turko-Mongol regimes in the fifteenth, sixteenth and seventeenth centuries. There were little prospect of controlling these unwieldy Khans until the nineteenth century. The fortifications that were built were not long-lasting because 'peace' was an ambiguous term that could be bought with the promise of exchange of lavish gifts and compensations but the Khans could not be sworn in to sign allegiance treaties. Moscow's 'entry' into Golden Horde territory was a myth in the practical sense. It was only in the eighteenth and nineteenth centuries that the nomad armies could be controlled through a series of artillery lines that blockaded supplies on the southern frontier. So, contrary to the image of an integrative frontier or voluntary submission of the nomads, Khodarkovsky described the frontier as distant and unwieldy where peace was impossible. His mind was preoccupied with Russian colonial interpretations of the steppe and its subjects as 'unfaithful' and 'ignoble savages'.[37]

Familiar but Distant: The Cossacks

The Turko-Mongol domain was a wide gamut and within this framework there were the Cossacks, the guardians of the Russian steppe territory in the west and acting as facilitators in the eastern barracks as far as the Altai.[38] Since the fifteenth century, the perilous and porous frontiers of Russia's south and the west were guarded by the Cossacks who were specialized military bands and often described in unflattering tones as 'freebooters'. They were the most prominent fighters on the western edge of the steppe frontier and were recruited by the Russian state in the fifteenth century to put a check on Turko-Mongol raiders of the steppe. So for the energetic Cossacks, fighting was the only way of life. According to claims made recently about the Cossacks' non-Russian influences, the Cossacks residing on the edge of the steppe were moving according to the rhythms of the steppe: they were a familiar part of the life on the frontier. They were professional soldiers—conditioned for war and working on their own account or hiring themselves out as soldiers in the various wars of the Turco-Mongol world of the steppe.[39] The Cossack enthusiasts argue that the Cossacks qualified as the *qazaqi* (Kazakhs), a claim which is however open to question. However, it is such claims that have unfolded a new dimension of the Cossack chapter in Eurasian history.

The origins of the Cossacks can be traced to the downfall of the Kipchak khanate in the fifteenth century. The inheritance of the khanate was claimed by the rival khanates of Kazan, Astrakhan and Crimea whose rulers time and again ravaged the settled lands north of the Volga and Dneiper rivers and carried off slaves for the Ottoman Empire. To guard the turbulent southern frontier, the Muscovite princes and the Slavic princes of Poland-Lithuania took the help of the Cossacks who knew the steppe intimately, ventured to any limit and excelled as soldiers of fortune who had no social ties whatsoever. They were continually hired as protectors of border towns who had the potential of combat *vis-à-vis* the dreaded Nogai warriors and the Tatars. Gradually the distance between the Turkic *qazaqi* and the Slavic frontiersmen (who had established themselves as adventurers in the *wild field*, tempted not only by the free life of the steppe but also by the potential of surplus trade in the fortress towns) waned and fortress Cossacks who had begun steadily serving the Grand Princes and the Polish kings and were getting inducted into regular military service soon developed a collective or group consciousness as they collaborated with the frontier people. They moved in and out of the steppe as a floating border population. Some of them also moved permanently into the steppe. Their trade was their name—being a Cossack—and it was they, the Turco-Mongolian *qazaqi*, who were changing the Slavic frontiersmen into something else and not vice versa.

In the early sixteenth century, the abolition of the political space of the Kipchak khanate resulted in a new dispensation:

the Cossacks coalesced into two organized communities on the Don and the Dneiper and claimed allegiance over the entire steppe territory inhabited by them. So the isolated bandit groups were transformed into proto-state units. The Muscovite and Polish princely authorities started collaborative work with this new group of activists to fend off the Nogai raid in the north. The organizational capacity of the Cossacks became legendary and the Cossacks on the Don and the Dneiper developed a sense of identity. The accounts of the Zaporozhian Cossacks (the Cossacks beyond the rapids) became extremely popular and the paramount control by the Cossack groups of the river system made them unbridled masters in the steppe's western territory.

The Cossack phenomenon in Eurasian history has been interpreted differently by different scholars. The Russian claim about the Cossacks as a service community is challenged by Ukrainian historians who argue that the Cossacks are central to their country's history more than Russia's.[40] The debate does not end there. Talking about how Russian imperial culture sustained through centuries, Christoph Witzenrath points out that it is the Siberian Cossacks' local activism that provided strength to the empire, not their servitude. The adaptability of the Cossacks in the steppe environs is amazing. What is also striking are the Cossack structures which made that adaptability easier. In a very novel treatment of the Siberian Cossacks' *personenverband*, a primary social group formation that was not based on kinship relations but on volition, Witzenrath highlights group activism among the members and a union that was based on common goals, not social status. It was a mechanism of self-protection in a wild, open steppe environment which was always vulnerable to Tatar attacks. Economic self-survival was also on the agenda: to store and stock enough surplus till winter and also to use that stock as bribes in the frontier towns where they primarily resided. So the *personenverband* did not represent individual interests, rather group interests. It was that group activism that could survive in competition with groups like the Tatars.[41] Witzenrath studies the role of the Siberian Cossacks, explaining how the institutions of the empire (the *voevodas* for instance) indulged them as traders in the big frontier towns of Yenisei, Tomsk and Irkutsk. The Siberian Cossacks carved out a niche for themselves in these towns not merely as *yasak* collectors of the Siberian Chancellery but also as traders of Siberian fur and sable which were in high demand in the international market. Soon, they emerged as local power brokers which intimidated the Russians. Restrictions on the *personenverband* resulted in internal regional tensions. Regionalism as an ideology and a phenomenon that developed in Siberia in the late nineteenth century and early twentieth century was an offshoot of the frontier federation mentality of the Siberian Cossacks, reincarnated as a motivated group that gradually degenerated as an 'ataman scourge' during the civil war period. With the revival of Siberian Cossacks' activism, attention shifts to the dynamism of steppe frontier culture. The overbearing dominance of literature on the Cossacks' military-administrative services was replaced by candid assertions about their multidimensional activities. They were not only premier horsemen but also servicemen with a lot of glamour. In Soviet studies, the special status of service communities of the seventeenth century has been treated with great care. The Cossacks belonged to this high profile group whose topgrade economic performance in European Russia made Soviet scholars attentive about the special services of the *voennosluzhilye lyudi*. The unification of Russia and Siberia gave them special opportunities as fiscal operators. Cossack trade service centres prospered in Tomsk, Kuznetsk, Nerchinsk *raions* and in the Yenisei-Krasnoyarsk *raion*.[42] Western impressions of the Cossacks as crude militarymen who were indulged by the Tsarist authorities as supervisors of the *ostrogi* (military detachments) and who mobbed the *starozhily* of their prized farmlands however seemed to pervade. The Cossack commanders hogged the limelight while the *starozhily* toiled as agriculturists and farmers trying to utilize their skills in every way possible, especially since the opening of the Trans-Siberian

Railroad and the reopening of the sea route which brought scores of European commercial agents via the Bering Sea to the Siberian waters of the Yenisei and the Lena.[43]

IMPRESSIONS OF SIBERIA

The steppe environment is a repertoire of sentiments. Retrospection about Siberia as paradise and *oblastnichestvo* as regional euphoria is evident in the 'new generation literature'. Recounting 'the new ways in Russian literature', Geoffrey Hosking referred to the contemplative mood of village prose writers like Valentin Rasputin and Vasily Shukshin.[44] Ideas that have gained ground are cultural perceptions about Siberia and its environment reflected in the Sibiriaks' imagining of a cultural landscape and their expressions about 'freedom' and 'people's will'. The images of Siberia as *volia* (free will)', as a pastoral, uncorrupted, spiritual landscape and a place of unrestricted space and complete individual freedom were getting appreciated.[45] Like their nineteenth-century mentors who wrote about their experiences in Siberian cities like Irkutsk recounting the joyful and enchanting atmosphere that was different from the gloomy world of the Russian capital of St. Petersburg,[46] a brave new generation of writers wrote about their homeland and disseminated to the world the all-pervading myth of Siberia as a threatened paradise. What gained attention is not the hostile environment of Siberia where bandits and raiders and Soviet daredevils left their mark but the century-old Siberia of angry rivers, icy cliffs and frozen deserts that symbolized Siberian identity and a Siberian landscape that is also part of the Eurasian steppe. These are 'plebeian' images of Siberia with the dominant view of Siberia as the 'ecological paradise'—a sharp contrast to the exiles' reflections about 'hell'. In Rasputin's words, 'Siberia is in no hurry to reveal itself and it placed its finest creations with love and good taste in its heartland.'[47] Vasily Shukshin (1929-74), an exiled filmmaker from the Altai region, wrote about the pristine beauty of rural settings. He missed his childhood days in Siberia and this led him to portray his protagonist as a *chudak* (eccentric) who was lost in his own world of music (*Odin*, 1963) or spent nights and weekends away from work. His 1966 composition *Okhota Zhit* (*I Want To Live*) was about an ex-convict who tries to escape his past and start afresh with honest work and a good companion. But his old gang traces him and kills him. Shukshin's subject matter was solitude as meaningful existence and not the drudgery of everyday life. To him, Siberia was a land of freedom (*volia*). The Siberian taiga did not represent the monolithic face of penal exile but a space for artistic freedom. His protagonist Nikitich, the convict who had taken shelter in the taiga, loved the place, specially the winter because 'the silence was so complete that it got him down a bit at times. But not the solitude. That gave him a sense of freedom. Nikitich would screw up his eyes and look around, knowing that he and he alone was master of this great white kingdom.'[48] This white kingdom, the taiga snow, was a distant paradise, a place that was a safe haven for those like the convict who wanted to redeem his life but had to meet a brutal end because his criminal past did not allow him to live.

The sublime setting of the taiga was so different from the public image of Siberia as a limitless space, wilderness, a remote terrain with lack of connectivity and a dumping ground for convicts and exiles, a region that disconnected men from their cozy locales. To the majority of exiles and deportees, Siberia as a colony was unattractive because it meant isolation from the motherland. The severe physical conditions were unbearable and made life unpleasant. What was also difficult to fathom was the cultural environment, represented by people of the steppe, both Russian as well as native. The Siberian wilderness was like a psychological bind for them: an inhospitable terrain, remote location and a metaphor of gloom. Those who were engaged in perilous projects along the war-torn Manchurian or Chinese frontiers of Siberia in the 1930s seemed to lack normal human values and feelings. Japan's proletarian writer Kuroshima Denji (1898-1943) felt Japanese militarymen lacked compassion, a quality one couldn't possibly learn to appreciate in the snows of Siberia. It was as if the brutal men were there to have fun, as if there was no law in Siberia.[49]

Like Siberia's plebian image, *oblastnichestvo's* charisma is a topic of unbounded interest which leads scholars of different generations to review it as a phenomenon. On the one hand, there is a short-sighted and limited view of *oblastnichestvo* as a movement for political autonomists of the revolutionary years. But there is also another approach that challenges hypothetical views about *oblastnichestvo* as a separatist movement or a movement of autonomy-seekers. In fact, there is enough evidence to prove that *oblastnichestvo* as a political variant was an illusion and that Buryat leaders were practically disillusioned by 1918. The activists' view of *oblastnichestvo* as a separatist movement is passé.[50] During the early years of perestroika, there were interesting publications about the *oblastniki's* multifaceted personality. One such publication analyses Yadrintsev's prose and poetry and Potanin's memoirs, indicating Yadrintsev's philosophical bent of mind and reflecting on Potanin's popularity as a keynote speaker in Siberian Dumas.[51] Another publication on the city profile points to the vibrant cultural-cum-economic landscape of railraod cities of Siberia. These cities, dominated by the mercantile elite, soon became the hub of *oblastniki* activity and the scene of dissemination of the *oblastniki's* ideas beyond the Pacific. Some of these ideas metamorphosed as research topics and determining the émigré character of *oblastnichestvo* is one major thrust of new-age writings. Recounting milestones in the development of *oblastnichestvo* as an émigré movement, Natalia Ablazhei has commented on the local particularities and the increasing demand for economic federalism.[52]

There is also an attempt to review Russian intellectual history, taking into account a generation of intellectuals who were indoctrinated by ideas of enlightenment and slavophilism and who were only concerned with the general good of all. Belonging to the elite intellectual group that was trained by Tsarist state institutions like Imperial Russian Geographical

Society were writers like Feodor Dostoevsky, scholar-enlightener Chokan Chingizovich Valikhanov, historian Afanasy Shchapov and ideologues G.N. Potanin and N.M. Yadrintsev. It is this rich intellectual tradition of the nineteenth century and the impact of their ideas that has been studied with great care. The patriotic fervour among regional historians like Leonid Goryushkin who took the initiative of continuing the Yadrintsev tradition in the present era has been acknowledged. Mikhail Shilovsky, the Novosibirsk historian, has studied the dominant phases of Russian intellectual history and his study represents Leonid Goryushkin as the trendsetter in this direction while V.G. Mirzoev as the other voice of the regionalist discourse who was concerned with local particularities. Mirzoev named forces of historical development, e.g. nature and climatic conditions of a particular region that determined human movement and migration patterns.

The discussion about human movement thus brings us back to Turner's thesis which is what the Siberian historians are preoccupied with. Shilovsky draws our attention to the development of *oblastnichestvo* as historical science. He re-examines the texts of the *oblastniki*, the atmosphere in which they were trained, and rebuilds the commentaries of critics to write his own guidebook about *oblastnichestvo* as an intellectual milieu which bonded people and their ideas about integration. Shilovsky's unique effort in this direction is to create a database of Siberian *oblastniki*. A collaborative group of Siberian historians with financial support from the Open Society-backed project at Pushkin Universal'nyi Scientific Library in Tomsk developed a website about Siberian regionalists, focusing on their biographies that give a fair sense about the wide range of their activities. The *oblastniki's* own experiences narrated through their memoirs and the dissemination of their ideas through letters of exchange have been carefully handled in this website which was invoked in 1999. Shilovsky has tried to globalize the Siberian phenomenon through various chapters in his website like *Sibirskie oblastniki* (comprising 'biographical sketches' of 20 *oblastniki*), *Khronika oblastnicheskovo dvizheniya v Sibirii (1852-1919), Elektronnye katalog Sibirskoe Oblastnichestvo*, and so on.[53] Shilovsky's works deal with Irkutsk and Tomsk as nerve centres of the *oblastniki*. I.I. Serebrennikov, one of the frontline regionalists, also highlighted these places as nodal centres that supervised the regional jurisdiction of caucus groups like the Siberian Regional Union, the Siberian Regional Duma, and so on.[54]

In the West too, there is similar interest in the *oblastnichestvo* as an intellectual movement. Wolfgang Faust was first among the Western writers who studied the *oblastnichestvo* in the overall context of an intellectual atmosphere. The inertia of the *oblastniki* is evident in Faust's writings about 'the first oppositionists' who were exiled out of Siberia. Faust's biographical study defines the social milieu of the *oblastniki* and has an approach that is very similar to the website project conceived by the Siberian collaborative group in Tomsk. Faust describes the public domain of the *oblastniki*. He characterizes the *oblastnichestvo* not as an organization or a party but a heterogeneous movement of the educated public of late nineteenth-century Siberia. In Faust's opinion, like many social reform movements, *oblastnichestvo* developed around a journal (*Vostochnoe Obozrenie*), a geographic society (*Imperatorskovo Russkovo Geographicheskovo Obshchestvo*) and local government institutions (Siberian Regional Duma).[55] Faust is not solely concerned with what the ideologues like Grigory Potanin and N.M. Yadrintsev propagated but what Siberian society at the turn of the century represented—transition. The Siberian regionalists, according to Faust, had in the first place imbibed ideas of Slavophilism and utopian socialism. But in the final analysis, they diverted to ideas and their ambitions about regional alternatives were different from the Great Russian populist thinking. In Faust's analysis, the regionalists were keen to experiment with situations as they came. So, from 1882 (when Yadrintsev wrote his polemic *Sibir' kak koloniya*) to the 1990s (since when Siberian regionalist historians are busy re-examining the economic possibilities of a federal accord), *oblastnichestvo* has come a long way. Discussions have revolved around how the Siberian movement was both adaptive and belligerent, adding emphasis on disparities between the Eastern hypothesis of the *oblastniki* and autonomy agendas of the Bashkirs and the Tatars.[56] Though primarily associated with the regional patriots of Russia of the late nineteenth century, *oblastnichestvo* came to be linked with the consciousness of other groups with differing loyalties. Regional concerns about educational reform, popularization of the regional press and increasing historical and anthropological knowledge of Russia's peripheries were on the ascendance and the classification of *oblastnichestvo* within the single rubric of autonomy became outdated. This re-examination had manifold properties and studies indicate the 'fluctuations' in the *oblastniki's* proposals over a span of 50 years. The heterogeneity of the concept came to full view during the post-revolutionary ardour of the SRs (social revolutionaries) and their adherents who advocated political programmes that had hardly anything in common with Yadrintsev's or Potanin's ideological concepts about Russia's land, man and nature. The dichotomous centre-periphery relations that was the pivotal issue in Yadrintsev's treatise *Sibir' kak koloniya* was somewhat redefined—twentieth-century advocates of Siberian regionalism became preoccupied with ideas about a federative structure in Russia. Claims of distinction and authority by the *oblastniki* through proposals of 'self-administration and economic management as the Russian local councils' (*zemstva*)[57] became unpopular. Critics have denounced the ambiguities that surfaced in the twentieth century and sealed the fate of *oblastnichestvo* as a political movement. The critique has added a new dimension to the form and content of *oblastnichestvo*. It has not only enriched the literature about *oblastnichestvo* but also raised questions about the hypothesis of *oblastnichestvo* as an autonomous movement with political ambitions only. The salience of cultural specificities of the east, the projection of the 'Eastern hypothesis' by the *oblastniki* and the emphasis on the eastern folklorist influence on the West are some features of this re-examination.[58]

REGIONOLOGY: AREA DYNAMICS

The re-examination of Eurasia as an integrative field has been pursued ardently by local scholars through their global journal *Central Asia and the Caucasus.* Founded in and supported by Sweden, the journal through its collaborative network all over the CIS has made a decisive attempt to focus on the structural components of Eurasia's new alignments. Most of these alignments tend to project Kazakhstan as an expanding economic zone with enormous potential that catered to the Russian, Chinese, Japanese or North Asian and South Asian interests. New names were given to these geopolitical groupings that were basically improvized versions of the 'Old World' and pointedly referred to the debates between the Russian geopolitical school (which tends to justify Russia's age-old imperial ambitions) and the alternatives or variants represented by adjacent territories. The Caucasus variant is one such category that is being addressed through such terms as 'Caucasasia' signifying the relevance of an Asian caucus juxtaposed to a pro-western Eurasian doctrine.[59] Japanese scholars too are focused on this alignment mechanism in Eurasia and have attributed special importance to the borderline CIS states. Their focus is on 'area dynamics' whereby they try to ascertain the distinctive features of a mega area and its satellites. The meso-mega area dynamics approach examines the mega area in the northern half of Eurasia, i.e. the former Soviet bloc and the East European regions that has changed dramatically since the collapse of the communist regimes due to massive political and economic upheavals. The change was analysed in the framework of a mega area, taking into consideration the diversity within this area even as people shared an identity based on common political, economic and historical experiences. A methodological terminology was applied to analyse the emerging regions and this was 'regionology'.[60] Since its inception in the 1990s, regionology has been preoccupied with examining not only institutional identity, but also self-identity and external identity. The idea that gained ground within the format of regionology is how regions reinvented themselves through these three sets of identities. This idea has translated itself as a specialized field of research among Japanese scholars affiliated to the Slavic Research Centre in Hokkaido. These scholars and their Russian collaborators have envisioned Slavic Eurasia as a mega-area and Central Eurasia and the Russian Far East as meso-areas and it is the dynamics of 'triadic relationships' (i.e. deviation, interaction and amalgamation) that acted as the lifeline that bonded them together.[61] Within the format of 'regionology' have been studied Russian regions east and south of the Urals with the focus on regional subsets that were integral not only to the imperial setting but also to the contemporary set-up. The growing attraction of the Russian Empire as a multinational space and the history of the Russian Empire have resulted in a critical examination of borderland histories. There is a certain methodological consensus within the academic community as historians have not only structured their arguments on empirical data about imperialism but have also begun considering new theories about critical space referring to debates within the realm of political geography and spatial geography, political economy, cultural nationalism, social anthropology, and so on. In their reappraisal of imperiology, Japanese scholars are attentive to the historical dynamics of macro-regions like the Volga Ural, Left Bank Ukraine, the steppe, western and eastern Siberia. Taking a bottom-up approach, these studies have immersed themselves in subjects that were largely left unattended, e.g. interactions between the imperial centre and macro-regions on the one hand and between macro-regions themselves that determined the course of imperial behaviour towards the areas mentioned above.[62] The integrative apparatus is therefore the most recent entry in Eurasian frontier studies. The idea is not to take a resistant view about the imperial centre which is stereotypically projected as the antagonistic other in nationalist narratives. Rather, the tendency is to assess empires as foundations, contexts and arenas within which several national projects interacted or competed. Here we see a reiteration of Kappeler's regional approach though 'imperiologists' have gone further to show the *actual interaction* in the regions.

The prominence of the Eurasian 'mega' project in Japan is reflected through the publications of Slavic Research Centre—mostly a collection of essays presented as individual presentations in the Centre's symposia and conferences on various aspects—(a) empire and nation-building, (b) history devalued, 'improvized' or revived, (c) cultural engagements reflected through daily practices and festivities, environment awareness of the Central Asians, Tatar intellectualism, sedentary-nomad lifestyles among the Uyghurs, Kazakhs and the Kyrgyz, cuisine bonanza among the oases settlers, the Zoroastrian practices among the Pamiris, and so on. Cultural studies depicting 'culture as discipline' also had this mega vision of interaction. In their assertions about culture being the abiding norm in every discursive aspect of social anthropology, scholars discussed the case of Russian anthropology and 'a mega cultural area' that developed with Europe as the locus and which finally shifted to Moscow.[63] The steppe's cultural domain is a subject of serious academic research and the findings of this domain are disseminated through the journal *Acta Slavica Iaponica*. Most writings in this journal are devoted to intellectual premises about the Eurasian frontier, reflecting optimism about emergent regions in the north and east of Eurasia. Research deals with the actual and not the proxy. There is more emphasis on future possibilities rather than missed opportunities. Hence, the eastern and northern borderlands of Eurasia have been attended to with great care. The journal's interpretation of regionalism in Russia is the following—regionalism as a progressive phenomenon and not a source of competition with the federal centre. Irina Busygina is assertive about Russia's regions that could emerge as active players, and not qualify merely as passive respondents of state policies.[64] It is important, according to the journal's spokesmen, for *krais* and *okrugs* to show more involvement and be less aggressive to their regional counterparts or be dependent on the federal centre, i.e. Moscow. They should have the ability to overcome their 'provincialisms' and take part in a regional programme even though there could be serious challenges. In the context of Siberia, the performance of regional economies becomes problematic because in such a vast setting, 'economic liabilities' have undermined new possibilities.

Nevertheless, it is Siberia and the Far East representing Russia's eastern maritime sector that have set the tone for new geopolitical partnerships and engagements in the Pacific coast. The history of maritime relationships that have evolved in the region has got a new lease of life since seminar programmes of Hokkaido have highlighted the economic dynamism of emerging areas. These relationships have been studied both from a historical and a contemporary perspective and the 'prospects' of multilateral triadic identities and federal governance in Russian regions east of the Urals are assessed. Various levels of competition between centrifugal and centripetal forces in Amur-Ussuri borderlands and mechanisms of transborder integration in Eurasia's eastern and northern borderlands have been assessed by Sapporo's academic groups.

The percolation of merchant capital into Siberia's provinces has rendered a special status to Siberia's mine-rich provinces like Barnaul and Tomsk. During the Soviet period there was a tradition of studying Eurasia's regional economies that were controlled and run by regional elites. Sapporo's Russian collaborators because of their Soviet background studied this subject intently and seemed to be vexed by the inconsistencies of Soviet policies in the provinces. The weakening of sectoral growth and discrepancies in the management of provincial economies during Stalin's time were considered to be factors that reduced the levels of economic performance and which were at the end, a matter of provincial politics. The grain crisis in Irkutsk in the NEP period was for instance triggered off by fierce inter-regional debates about grain procurement. Such internal pressures were also felt in the contemporary period in regions like Krasnoyarsk and Tyumen.[65] In the post-disintegration period, there have been signs of economic opportunism in Tyumen *oblast*, the main oil and gas reserve, Omsk *oblast* which is a major oil refinement centre and in Krasnoyarsk *krai* which is a metallurgy base though surprisingly, these regions were noteworthy in the late nineteenth century as self-sufficient units that were connected by railroads and water roads with the markets of Europe and America and were showcased as sites for Western entrepreneurs and travellers who were actively engaged in mining projects of western Siberia. As business tension in these regions increased in the 1990s and early years of the twenty-first century, there was more and more speculation about the endurance of Russia's protective policies.[66]

CONCLUSION

Reflections of this kind indicate multidisciplinary approaches regarding frontiers and borderlands. In a globalized landscape, social scientists have reoriented themselves more and more towards moving frontiers as a renewed field of enquiry. There is a tendency to replace the traditional image of spatiality. The focus at present is on the edges as critical spaces that have been reformatted as dominant settings. Frontiers no longer mean confined territorial spaces, but human spaces. The impact of these human spaces on the surroundings and vice versa is not only a discursive aspect but a reality that has been addressed by post-disintegration literature. The steppe as a specimen of this human environment has acquired some attention.

NOTES

1. Historians have been engaged in discerning the methodologies of Russian and Soviet history. The importance of borderlands history has been indicated in theme-based issues of the journal *Kritika: Explorations in Russian and Eurasian History.* The articles that refer to research trends, shifts in historiography, etc., are 'The Imperial Turn', *Kritika,* 7, 4, 2006, pp. 705-12; G.M. Hamburg, 'Imperial Entanglements: Two New Histories of Russia's Western and Southern Borderlands', *Kritika,* 9, 2, Spring 2008.

2. Frederick Jackson Turner, 'The Significance of the Frontier in American History'. His essays (republished in 1920) are available in the website http://xroads.virginia.edu/~Hyper/TURNER.
3. Literature on the subject is vast. Examples: Daniel R. Brower and Edward Lazzerini, *The Russian Orient: Imperial Borderlands and Peoples, 1750-1917*, Bloomington: I.B. Tauris, 1997; Mark Bassin, *Imperial Vision: Nationalist Imagination and Geographical Expansion in the Russian Far East, 1840-1865*, Cambridge: Cambridge University Press, 1999; Mikhail Khodarkovsky, *Russia's Steppe Frontier: The Making of a Colonial Empire, 1500-1800*, Bloomington: Indiana University Press, 2002; Andreas Kappeler, 'Yuzhniy I vostochnyi frontir Rossii', *Ab Imperio*, no. 1, 2003. These and other works are cited in Alfred Rieber, 'Changing Concepts and Constructions of Frontiers: A Comparative Historical Approach', in *Ab Imperio*, no. 1, 2003.
4. Dietrich Gerhard, 'The Frontier in Comparative View', *Comparative Studies in Society and History*, vol. 1, no. 3, March 1959; William T. Rowe, 'Owen Lattimore, Asia and Comparative History', *The Journal of Asian Studies*, vol. 66, no. 3 (August), 2007.
5. The voluminous work of nineteenth-century Russian historian Sergei Mikhailovich Solovev (1820-79) (a 29-volume *History of Russia from the Earliest Times*), restored as a 15-volume Soviet edition (1959-66), was a national saga of Russian historical development. Solovev metaphorically described Russia's growth in terms of a social organism that grew and matured just as a human embryo.
6. Research about Siberia's frontiers and interaction among settler groups especially in the Tomsk *guberniya*, is considerable. Some useful references are D. Ya Rezun, *Frontir v istorii sibiri I severnoi Ameriki v XVII-XX vekov: obschee I osobennoe*, Vypusk 3, Novosibirsk, 2003; T.S. Mamisk, 'Povo'lzhe I Priob'e: Ochagi rannevo kulturnovo vzaimodeistviya, XVII-seredina XIX vek', *Sibirskii plavil'ny kotel: sotsial'no-demograficheskie protsessi v Severnoi Azii XVI-nachala XX veka, Sbornik nauchnoi statei*, Novosibirsk, 2004. These and other works cited in D.A. Ananyev et al., *"Novye Zemli" i osvoennie Sibri v XVII-XIX veke: ocherki istorii I istoriografii*, Novosibirsk, 2006.
7. M.V. Shilovsky, 'Sibirskii frontir: neokonchennoe puteshestvie po neizveddanoi zemle', *Evraziia: regionalnye perspektivy: sbornik materialov mezhdunarodnoi nauchnoi konferentsii 1-4 Iuniya 2007 godu*, Novosibirsk: Sibirskoe Nauchnoe Izdatel'stvo, 2007.
8. The comparison is obvious mainly because of Lattimore's Chinese background. He spent his early childhood in China where he lived, after education abroad, almost continuously between 1919-42. During this period, he travelled widely in Xinjiang, Mongolia and Manchuria. He started his career as an itinerant commercial agent in Mongolia

and subsequently turned to academic, political and diplomatic work. He made significant contributions as journalist and travel writer and ultimately became a foreign policy commentator joining the History Department at John Hopkins University in 1937. He was not a trained historian but he was attracted to the academic circuit of geographers and historians who were influenced by the idea of ecological influences on human and social development. Lattimore's mentor was Wittofogel who in 1931 wrote about China as a 'hydraulic society' and the awesome power of the state and bureaucracy. Wittofogel analysed China's exclusive history, shorn of the parameters of progressive stages in the West. Lattimore followed K.A. Wittofogel (though he disassociated himself from his mentor later in the 1930s), arguing ecology as the fundamental determinant of the history of human groups. Therefore, Lattimore was nurtured in the inter-war years of social science and the atmosphere of debate surrounding ecology and environment, the impact of terrain and climate on human behaviour.

9. Owen Lattimore, *Inner Asian Frontiers of China*, Hong Kong: Oxford University Press, 1988 (republished version), Part I, Chapter I.
10. There is a tendency to compare the two perspectives. Lattimore's frontier discourse begins with an analysis of eastern frontiers while Turner exclusively refers to America's wild frontier that modified with time. Turner's analysis of the American frontier as a specimen was very different from Owen Lattimore who spoke about the frontier as a world space. The hypotheses of Lattimore and Turner, representing two different perspectives, have inspired generations of writers for offering a new dimension of knowledge—the knowledge about the frontier as a vibrant, dynamic society and not a distant location representing wilderness or desolation. Lattimore and Turner popularized frontier history as living history or moving history as both spoke about people and their habitat.
11. Owen Lattimore, 'Caravan Routes of Inner Asia', in *Studies in Frontier History: Collected Papers, 1928-58, Part I: The Inner Asian Frontier,* London: Oxford University Press, 1962.
12. For example: Owen Lattimore, 'At the Crossroads of Inner Asia', *Pacific Affairs,* vol. 23, no. 1, March 1950.
13. Owen Lattimore, *Inner Asian Frontiers of China*, Hong Kong: Oxford University Press, 1988, p. 529.
14. Lattimore's ideas about interactive zones of China were revived by another Sinologist David Christian. David Christian, *A History of Russia, Central Asia and Mongolia: Inner Eurasia from Prehistory to the Mongol Empire*, vol. I, Oxford: Blackwell, 1998.
15. Lattimore was influenced by the ideas of William Morris Davis, Ellsworth Huntington, Isaiah Bowman—all belonging to the new

school of thinking about human geography and the history of human groups and their habitats. Their ideas about ecology and society, civilization and culture, technology and production were adopted and repudiated by Lattimore to conceptualize his own frontier model. William Rowe, op. cit., pp. 761-5.

16. Examples are Morris Rossabi, *China and Inner Asia: From 1368 to the Present Day*, New York: Pica Press, 1975; Nicola Di Cosmo, *Ancient China and its Enemies: The Role of Nomadic Power in East Asian History*, Cambridge: Cambridge University Press, 2002; William T. Rowe, 'Approaches to Modern Chinese Social History', in Olivier Zunz (ed.), *Reliving the Past: the Worlds of Social History*, Chapel Hill: University of North Carolina Press, 1985; Daniel Power and Naomi Standen (eds.), *Frontiers in Question: Eurasian Borderlands, 700-1700*, St. Martin's Press, 1999; Andreas Kappeler, 'Yuzhniy I vostochnyi frontir Rossii', *Ab Imperio*, no. 1, 2003; M.V. Shilovskii, 'Frontir i pereseleniya', *Frontir I istorii Sibirii I severnoi Ameriki v 17-20 vekov: obshchee I osobennoe, Sbornik nauchnoi statei*, Novosibirsk, 2003; Andreas Kappeler, 'Yuzhniy I vostochnyi frontir Rossii', *Ab Imperio*, no. 1, 2003.
17. Christoph Witzenrath, *Cossacks and the Russian Empire, 1598-1725: Manipulation, Rebellion and Expansion into Siberia*, London: Routledge, 2007; Shane O' Rourke, *The Cossacks*, Manchester: Manchester University Press, 2007.
18. The world of Islamic publishing in Central Asia unfolds the myth of a loose fabric of Muslim spirituality in Kazakhstan. The oral tradition of disseminating Islamic knowledge among the Kazakhs is perhaps well known. What is less obvious is the character of Islamic publishing in Kazakh urban settings of Almaty and Turkistan. The availability of Islamic booklets and pamphlets in the *bazaars* of Almaty and Turkistan is a striking feature of religiosity in Kazakhstan.

    The Muslim institutional activity in Kazakhstan is another aspect of Frank's studies on steppe religion. 'Introduction', in Allen J. Frank, *Popular Islamic Literature in Kazakhstan: An Annotated Bibliography*, Hyattsville: Dunwoody Press, 2007; Allen J. Frank, *Muslim Religious Institutions in Imperial Russia: the Islamic World of Novouzensk District and the Kazakh Inner Horde, 1780-1910*, Leiden: Brill, 2001.
19. There is overall recognition of the Kazakhs' Turkic identity while the Kazakhs' Muslim affiliation is almost a given, though not spoken very widely in cities like Almaty where the Kazakhs feel more close to the Russians. This may have been the result of Soviet propagation but what can't be taken very lightly are early writings about the Kazakhs' religiosity. Chokan Valikhanov was first among his contemporaries who gave an insider's view of Kazakh religion. He was the first Kazakh

ethnographer who studied Kazakh spiritual traditions and reported on intricate details of shamanism as a pre-Islamic faith in Inner Asia. Valikhanov's information on how the Kazakhs lived and practised several faiths has been a source of inspiration for most ethnographers today. Bruce G. Privratsky, *Muslim Turkistan: Kazak Religion and Collective Memory*, Richmond, Surrey: Curzon, 2001.

20. Denis Sinor, *The Cambridge History of Early Inner Asia*, Cambridge: Cambridge University Press, 1990, pp. 3-14.
21. 'Introduction' in Reuven Amitai and Michael Biran (eds.), *Mongols, Turks and Others: Eurasian Nomads and the Sedentary World*, Leiden: E.J. Brill, 2005.
22. David Morgan indulges in a source-based study of the *yasa* taking into account the Persian sources and reconstructing them in the light of subsequent revelations, e.g. *The Secret History of the Mongols* (1980) and Rashid al Din's *Jami al-tawarikh*. David Morgan, 'The Great "Yasa" of Chingiz Khan' and the Mongol Ilkhanate', *Bulletin of the School of Oriental and African Studies*, University of London, vol. 49, no. 1, in Honour of Ann K.S. Lambton, 1986; David Morgan, 'The "Great *Yasa* of Chinggis Khan" Revisited', in Reuven Amitai and Michael Biran (eds.), *Mongols, Turks and Others, Eurasian Nomads and the Sedentary World*, Leiden: E.J. Brill, 2005, p. 292.
23. Stephen Kotkin, 'Mongol Commonwealth? Exchange and Governance Across the Post-Mongol Space', *Kritika: Explorations in Russian and Eurasian History*, 8, 3, Summer 2007. Later cited as 'Mongol Commonwealth'.
24. Kotkin, 'Mongol Commonwealth', p. 519.
25. Peter Finke, 'Changing Property Rights System in Mongolia', *Max Planck Institute for Social Anthropology Working Papers*, Working Paper no. 3, Halle/Salle, 2000.
26. Cited in the introduction of Reuven Amitai and Michael Biran (eds.), *Mongols, Turks and Others: Eurasian Nomads and the Sedentary World*, Leiden: E.J. Brill, 2005.
27. Editorial 'Probing the Limits of Historical Metanarratives: Imperial Boundaries', *Ab Imperio*, 1, 2003.
28. Tatyana Skrynnikova, 'Russia in Buryats' identity construction'; Sergei Abashin, 'The Archaeology of Central Asian Nationalisms', *Ab Imperio*, 1, 2003.
29. Elena Bezvikonnaia, 'Geopolitical Space of the Steppe: The Omsk Region and the Problem of the Frontier in Russian Imperial Statebuilding', *Ab Imperio*, 1, 2003.
30. Suzanne Wertheim, 'Language Ideologies and the Purification of Post-Soviet Tatar', *Ab Imperio*, 1, 2003.
31. David Laitin, 'What is a Language Community?', *Ab Imperio*, 1, 2003.

32. Andreas Kappeler, 'Yuzhnyi I vostochnyi frontir Rossii', *Ab Imperio*, no. 1, 2003, p. 47.
33. Kappeler has always spoken about a range of ideas, a span of thinking. In another essay where he has reviewed opposing views of the empire and the periphery in Soviet and post-Soviet historiographies, Kappeler shows that the periphery was always misrepresented. A comprehensive history of the peripheries of Russia's empire was almost impossible to find during the Soviet period. A Russia-dominated narrative harmonized imperial conquest and assimilation with the 'progressive union' of non-Russian peripheries. Writers commissioned for writing encyclopaedias and histories that reflected a *sovetskyi soyuz* model excluded and included peripheries in their works. The nationalist historiographies of the 1990s were ethnocentric and imagined the great past of the Golden Horde, the Tatar intellectuals, the Uzbek *jadid* movement without caring to refer to other significant phases and actors. So, even among regional historians there were differences of opinion. Andreas Kappeler, 'The Russian Empire and its Nationalities in Post-Soviet Historiographies', in Hayashi Todayuki (ed.), *The Construction and Deconstruction of National Histories in Slavic Eurasia*, Sapporo, 2003.
34. Mikhail Khodarkovsky, *Russia's Steppe Frontier: The Making of a Colonial Empire, 1500-1800*, Bloomington: Indiana University Press, 2002, Chapter 1.
35. Ibid., p. 25.
36. Ibid., p. 156.
37. Ibid., concluding chapter, pp. 221-9.
38. Thomas Witlam Atkinson, *Oriental and Western Siberia, A Narrative of Seven Years Explorations and Adventures in Siberia, Mongolia, the Kirghiz Steppes, Chinese Tartary and Part of Central Asia*, Philadelphia: J.W. Bradley, 1859 [reprinted by Asian Educational Services, New Delhi, 2000], Chapters XI, XII, XIII.
39. Shane O' Rourke, *The Cossacks*, Manchester: Manchester University Press, 2007, p. 29.
40. Mykhailo Hrushevsky, *History of the Ukrainian Cossacks: From Pre-history to the Eleventh Century*, tr. Marta Skorupsky and ed. Andrzej Poppe, Edmonton and Toronto: Canadian Institute of Ukrainian Studies Press, 1997.
41. Christoph Witzenrath, *Cossacks and the Russian Empire, 1598-1725: Manipulation, Rebellion and Expansion into Siberia*, London: Routledge, 2007, pp. 34-7.
42. V.A. Aleksandrov, 'Voisko-organizatsiya sibirskikh sluzhylykh lyudei XVII veka', *Istoriya SSSR*, no. 3, 1988; N.E. Nikitin, 'Voennosluzhiliye lyudi I Sibiri v XVII veke', *Istoriya SSSR*, no. 2, 1980.

43. Inputs from M.P. Price, *Siberia (Siberian Discovery Series,* Vol. 6), The Quadrant, Richmond: Curzon, 2000 and M.A. Czaplicka's *My Siberian Year (David Collins edited Collected Works of M.A. Czaplicka)*, vol. 3, The Quadrant, Richmond: Curzon, 1999.
44. Geoffrey Hosking, 'The Twentieth Century: In Search of New Ways, 1953-80', in Charles A. Moser (ed.), *The Cambridge History of Russian Literature*, Cambridge: Cambridge University Press, 1989.
45. This was expressed by Archpriest Avvakum Petrovich (1620-82), in *The Life Written by Himself.* Bruce T. Holl, 'Avvakum and the Genesis of Siberian Literature', in Galya Diment and Yuri Slezkine (eds.), *Between Heaven and Hell: The Myth of Siberia in Russian Culture*, New York: St. Martin's Press, 1993.
46. Galya Diment, 'Exiled *from* Siberia: The Construction of Siberian Experience by Early Nineteenth Century Irkutsk Writers', in Galya Diment and Yuri Slezkine (eds.), *Between Heaven and Hell: The Myth of Siberia in Russian Culture*, New York: St. Martin's Press, 1993, p. 60.
47. Valentin Rasputin, *Siberia, Siberia* [tr. with an introduction by Margaret Winchell and Gerald Mikkelsen], Evanston, Illinois: Northwestern University Press, 1996, p. 61.
48. Translation of Vasily Shukshin's *I want to Live* (1966) in *Soviet Literature*. Website: www.sovlit.com/rasskazy/iwanttolive.html
49. The brutality comes to full view in the numbing descriptions of Stalinist repressions in 1933—the deportation camps of Nazino Island in western Siberia. Nicolas Werth's *Cannibal Island: Death in a Siberian Gulag* (2007) describes the plight of the deportees who were city dwellers and were labelled as kulaks and 'special settlers' representing several ethnic groups. The 'déclassé and socially harmful elements' were left to their fate on the little island that stood at the confluence of the Ob and the Nazina rivers, about 800 km north of the Siberian city of Tomsk.
50. Dina Amanzhalova, 'The Movement for Siberian Regional and National Autonomy in the Early 1920s', *Sibirica*, 3, no. 1, 2003.
51. N. Yanovskii, *Pisateli Sibiri (izbrannie stati)*, chapters 'Vernye Syny Sibiri' ['Proza I poeziya N.M. Yadrintseva', 'O vospominanyakh G.N. Potanina'], Moscow: Sovremennik, 1988.
52. N.N. Ablazhei, *Sibirs'koe oblastnichestvo v emigratsii*, Novosibirsk: Institute of Archaeology and Ethnography, RAN, 2003.
53. http://oblastnichestvo.lib.tomsk.ru/page.php?id=2
54. I.I. Serebrennikov, 'The Siberian Autonomous Movement and its Future', *The Pacific Historical Review*, vol. 3, no. 4, December 1934.
55. Wolfgang Faust, *Russlands goldener Boden: Der sibirsche regionalismus in der zweiten halfte des 19. Jahnhunderts*, Cologne: Bohlau, 1980.

Review of Faust's monograph by Mark von Hagen in *Russian Review*, vol. 41, no. 1, January 1982.

56. Despite activism among the Sibiriaks and autonomy as the motivating factor behind collaboration between *oblastniki* and anti-Bolshevik Kazakh and Bashkir activists, there were regional peculiarities and debates during the Civil War period indicating the rift among the Sibiriaks.
57. Amanzhalova, op. cit., p. 92.
58 Elena Kovalaschina, 'The Historical and Cultural Ideals of the Siberian *Oblastnichestvo*', *Sibirica*, 6, issue 2 (Autumn 2007).
59. Vladimir Papava, 'Central Caucasasia Instead of Central Eurasia', *Central Asia and the Caucasus*, no. 2 (50), 2008, pp. 35-42.
60. Osama Ieda, 'Regional Identities and Meso-Mega Area Dynamics in Slavic Eurasia: Focussed on Eastern Europe', in Kimitaka Matsuzato (ed.), *Emerging Meso Areas in the Former Socialist Countries: Histories Revived or Improvised?*, Sapporo: Slavic Research Center, Hokkaido University, 2005, pp. 19-33. Ieda's methodological approach cited by Alexei Voskressenski, 'Regional Studies in Russia and Current Methodological Approaches for Social/Historical/Ideological [Re]construction of International Relations and Regional Interaction in Eastern Eurasia', Ieda Osamu and Uyama Tomohiko (eds.), *Reconstruction and Interaction of Slavic Eurasia and its Neighbouring Worlds*, Sapporo: Slavic Research Centre, 2006.
61. Ideas of a geostrategic triad envisioned by Z. Brzezinski, *The Geostrategic Triad: Living with China, Europe and Russia*, Washington: The CSIS Press, 2002.
62. Kimitaka Matsuzato, 'Introduction' in *Imperiology: From Empirical Knowledge to Discussing Empire*, 21st Century Salvic Eurasian Studies no. 13, Sapporo: Slavic Research Center, Hokkaido University, 2007, pp. 7-8.
63. Marina Mogilner, 'The Most European Science in Russia: Defining the Empire Anthropologically', Kimitaka Matsuzato (ed.), *Emerging Meso Areas in the Former Socialist Countries: Histories Revived or Improvised?'*, Sapporo: Slavic Research Center, Hokkaido University, 2005, pp. 293-5.
64. Irina Busygina, 'Russia's Regions in Search of Identity', *Acta Slavica Iaponica*, issue 19, 2002.
65. James Hughes, *Stalin, Siberia and the Crisis of the New Economic Policy*, Cambridge: Cambridge University Press, 1991; Hughes, *Stalinism in a Russian Province: A Study of Collectivization and Dekulakization in Siberia*, Basingstoke and London: Macmillan Press in association with the Centre for Russian and East European Studies, University of Burmingham, 1996.

66. Andrew Yorke, 'Business and Politics in Krasnoyarsk *Krai*', *Europe-Asia Studies*, vol. 55, no. 2, 2003; Neil J. Melvin, 'The Consolidation of a New Regional Elite: The Case of Omsk 1987-1995', *Europe-Asia Studies*, vol. 50, no. 4, 1998; Pete Glatter, 'Continuity and Change in the Tyumen Regional Elite 1991-2001', *Europe-Asia Studies*, vol. 55, no. 3, 2003; Joachim Zweynert, 'Economic Ideas and Institutional Change: Evidence from Soviet Economic Debates 1987-1991', *Europe-Asia Studies*, vol. 58, no. 2, March 2006.

CHAPTER 2

The Kazakh Story

INTRODUCTION: THE KAZAKH DYNAMICS

The steppe dynamics in Eurasia and the subsistence model of nomadic pastoralism is best represented by Kazakhstan. In post-Soviet literature about Kazakhstan, the combination of historical and anthropological views has led to an understanding of the nomadic environment of a particular ethnic group that moved annually with its animals from one seasonal pasture to another. The vague notion of the Kazakhs as freebooters who wandered from place to place has been replaced by an understanding of the social organization (nomadic pastoralism) to which they belonged and to the pattern of movements that were not random in nature but occurred in a sequence and most usually within a defined territory where pastures for grazing were available. These nomadic groups also maintained a relationship of exchange with the sedentary economies that surrounded them. The adaptability of the nomads and their interaction with the sedentary people are issues that have been discussed often and the Kazakh-Russian symbiotic relationship became the model of a steppe tradition of 'tolerance' that was rhetorically argued by the Nazarbayev government. This preoccupation with a permissive surrounding had a recuperative effect, especially after a slow process of Kazakhization[1] that had made the non-Kazakhs wary of a nationalist upsurge. Some sociologists began to question the nation-building project from the standpoint of a citizenship status after Kazakhstan announced the 'in gathering' that invites ethnic Kazakhs (*oralmany*) from various countries to resettle within the territory of the newly independent country and homeland of Kazakhstan.[2] As in the rest of Central Asia and the CIS states, the zeal of toleration spread and there were newer approaches towards state-society relations as well as inter-group relations.[3]

The changing equations between combative and collaborative groups are a recurrent feature of post-Soviet literature on Kazakhstan. There were reflections of the Kazakh mind and the quality of endurance among the Kazakhs was highlighted. Social harmony became a catchy phrase and the adaptive principles among Kazakh tribes were emphasized as belonging to historical tradition. The acceptance of Russian colonial administration by the Kazakh khans was specially discussed. The longstanding Kazakh tradition of reconciliation with competing power groups, the Kazakh tradition of leadership and control bequeathed to successive generations of *batyrs* (heroes), *biys* (governors) and *sultans* by powerful Kazakh tribal chieftains belonging to the Golden Horde and the Middle Horde—i.e. a tradition that had not withered despite colonial machinations of the nineteenth century, were emphasized. The Kazakhs' nationalist historiography focused on the reinvention of legacies. A series of personalities, their family histories and career graphs that influenced colonial policies were brought to life. The orientation was more towards 'enlightenment' and 'integration' rather than encounter and conflict. The authority's stance of a renewal of the social base was immediately approved by elite academic groups and historians took the lead in affirming *a people's history*.[4] The harmony model was also applied by sociologists who discussed how solidarity groups within the *avlod*, *mahalla*, *qaum* and *oila* (local terms, equivalent of 'community') functioned.[5]

But there were nuances in this rhetoric of toleration and the political slogan of diversity was not accepted wholeheartedly. President Nazarbaev's proclamation of a supraethnic

Kazakh community, i.e. *qazaq ulty*, on 31 August 2004 was political jargon that failed to impress a majority of non-Kazakhs who apprehended a shift to assimilation tactics by the Kazakh government. Critics felt that negative effects of such supraethnic consolidation policies were imminent. All Kazakh citizens had the right to feel equal and be at the core of the system. Hence, the political pronouncement of the president did not give them that assurance and surprisingly the Russians, despite centuries of Russification, felt threatened and there were rumours about their minority status.[6] The academia's response was negative—scholars were of the opinion that such attempts at segregation of a prime group would result in a backlash and increase groupism among the Russians and a contestation with Kazakh linguistic groups was bound to happen.

Such strains in society became evident in actual debates that started after the president's proclamation. Language became a contentious issue in Kazakhstan and since 2005 intellectuals expressed their reservations about consolidation of a Kazakh nation on the basis of language. The Russians too reacted to the situation through the Cossack cultural association *Lad* which continues to remain a strong Russian voice[7] though marginalized in the Kazakh arena. *Russkaya Obshchina* on the other hand has collaborated more effectively with Nazarbayev's government.

As the euphoria of social harmony fizzled out, there was a tendency to review power relationships in the steppe. Research reached out to new arenas of a steppe ecumene like environment and ecology. There was an attempt to combine the global discourse about nomadism with the Kazakhs' tribal culture. The use of the tribal discourse in scientific discourse, especially in natural sciences is a new aspect of the revivalist historiography in Kazakhstan. The historian Nurbulat Masanov was openly supportive of the new science-based arguments and pursued the relevance of the archaeological thematic. In his view, the sphere of nomadic control is crucial to an understanding of the dynamics of pastoral nomadism. Inherent to the steppe specimen were not only nomadic traits of the Kazakhs, Kyrgyz and the Mongols inhabiting Semirechie territory but also the mechanism of tribal order, rejuvenation of nomad political organization through judicial reforms during the regime of Tauke Khan (1689-1717), and migratory patterns among Turkic groups after Mongol interference. How all these were affected by the imperial statutes of the nineteenth century were also considered. But primary attention was given to key issues of rupture—exercise of legality and control over collective rights (e.g. land) and individual rights (e.g. cattle). Simultaneously, the diffusion of a Kazakh voice became a key aspect of the new analysis. Dissent and rebellion in the nineteenth century and the spectacle of revolt in 1916 in the aftermath of 'dramatic transformation' of the Kazakh economy as a cash belt, the genesis of a secular world-view among educated Kazakhs, the origins of 'imperial deputations' from Kazakhstan, the spread of alternative thinking among Kazakh Muslim intellectuals and the emergence of the movement for *Alash* (unity) and the significance of the Alash Orda movement (1905-17) are some aspects of the new historical analysis.

There were thus twists in the tale and Soviet and post-Soviet Kazakh historiographies have dealt with episodic aspects of Kazakh history. There were different styles of writing and local histories of the region were interpreted differently. On the one hand there was a plethora of sentiments that merged on to a colonial setting. On the other hand, speculations about Kazakh and non-Kazakh (Chinese, Uyghurs, Mongols, Germans and Poles) relations grew over time. Relational patterns within the tribal structures were also discussed that gave a boost to the image of pastoral nomadism.

STEPPE POLITICAL TRADITION

Over the years, general accounts of pastoral nomadism and the extent of their influence on the sedentary world have increased considerably. These accounts have challenged the stereotypical image of a binary opposition between the nomad and the settler and have showcased the interactive world of the nomads and their sedentary partners and the range of cultural influence stretching from Hungary and Poland to Iran, Ukraine, Russia, China, Mongolia, India and Egypt. Impressions about shared characteristics of the socio-economic tribal federation represented by the fifteenth-century Kazakhs or the thirteenth-century Mongols, the pedigree-status of nomad Turks in the Islamic sedentary courts of medieval India despite critical assessments about 'detribalization' or 'denomadization' of the frontier areas have popularized Khazanov's sociological parameters.[8] In Soviet and post-Soviet representations of Kazakh history too, we find considerable efforts to restore the image of Kazakh nomadism. The Kazakh historian who idealized the Kazakhs' sociological structure was Nurbulat Masanov (1954-2006). His ardent Indian disciple Bhavna Dave supports Masanov as a sociologist who adopted Kazakh genealogy as a tool to define the Kazakh power structure. Masanov 'referred to a pervasive cult of seniority among the nomads, a cult that was produced by genealogical knowledge and memory (the ability to remember the *shezhire* [genealogy]) and revolved around demonstrating the position of one's segment in the historical chain of lineage in order to claim pre-eminence'.[9] Masanov's genealogical claims are reiterated by a Western scholar, Hilda Eitzen. Her account is about multiple registers of genealogy in the Kazakh-Uzbek tribal confederation, some of which disappeared as the Kazakhs moved and migrated to new settlements since the fifteenth century. The genealogies were fragile, some of them eclipsed but most of them were preserved because of the migration of the tribes. There is evidence of the *zhuz* (clan or tribal group) nomenclature across Central and Inner Asia in regions as diverse as the Volga, Caucasus, Bashkiria, eastern Afghanistan and Crimea. In assertions about Kazakhness, there is also reference to some of these tribal legacies reclaiming Turkic affiliations and identities that are common not only to Inner Asian tribal groups but extend up to the Near East and Europe.[10]

The ruptures within the tribal confederation did not signify an end to the tribal political tradition. Masanov's predecessor S.E. Tolybekov, a leading exponent of Soviet Union's Central Asian historiography, provided an insider's view of the development of Soviet sociology, taking immense pride in the effects of 'modernization' on Kazakh society and recounting milestones in the symbiotic relationship between a 'semi-nomadic Kazakh society' and a 'patriarchal settled one'. Tolybekov noted that in the Kazakh nomadic system there was a combination of various traits. Every illiterate nomadic Kazakh, Tolybekov said, was, during the fifteenth to eighteenth centuries, simultaneously a shepherd and a soldier, an orator and a historian, a poet and a singer. Tolybekov's judgement was based on the Russo-centric notion of the benefits of Russian colonization for the Kazakh people.[11]

Discussions have touched upon other aspects of nomadic dispensation though it is the political economy of nomadism that is central to all discussions. The Kazakhs are primarily associated with their *zhuz* legacy that is reminiscent of tribal affiliations. But in the 1990s saw a wave of writings on other important aspects of steppe tradition. For instance, in 1998, *Nationalities Papers* published its special issue on Kazakhstan in which Kazakh and non-Kazakh scholars shared their convictions about the Khan's leadership qualities while participation in the will and the instruction of the *tengri* (sky) were important attributes of political authority. The wisdom of the *kagan* (Khan), his ability to honour values gives him a special place in his tribe. The nomad leader is expected to be chivalrous, but more important is his political genius to perpetuate control of his tribe. Chingiz Khan was the trendsetter and the laws of succession and inheritance codified in his *yasa* (order) account for the durability of his regime. The power of union, demonstrated by the *quriltay* (Congress) was another aspect of political tradition in the steppe.[12] This also leads to introspection about other intricate patterns and inter-tribal relations, e.g. the Kazakhs' relations with members of the tribal confederation who inhabited the Dasht-i-Kipchak area. So, the Uzbek leanings of a Kazakh from Turkestan are as strong as the Uighur or Usun legacy of a Kazakh residing in the Chinese borderland. The Kazakhs' memories are associated with their origins in the Dasht-i-Kipchak area, also the home of the Uzbek Shaibanids which was besieged in the sixteenth century by the powerful Kazakh chieftain Kasym Khan. The latter ousted all rival tribal chiefs in the west and the east (especially the Nogais) and rejuvenated the 'tribal home' of the three *zhuzes* that also spread out in the direction of the Dzhungar stronghold in the east. It is interesting to note that such migrations in the past have generated a combination of genealogies and Hilda Eitzen's study about genealogies among the Kazakhs with multiple affiliations to the Naiman, the Uzbek, the Nogai among the Kazakhs has reinforced this argument.

The spread of genealogical histories has been examined by many other post-Soviet studies. An example is the study that has traced the Nogai Horde lineage in western Kazakhstan, in the steppe region between the rivers Emba and Yaik, which was conventionally regarded as Golden Horde territory. But according to the testimony of Persian and Turkic chronicles, this region passed under Middle Horde control (under Altytuly *ulus* (clan)) and the Nogai aristocrats (*mirzas*) became the prime masters after they won the tussle for power with other subjugated nomadic groups. The apparatus of political control exercised by the Altytuly *mirzas* throughout the sixteenth and seventeenth centuries is a significant chapter in the political history of the steppe. Not only did the *mirzas* strengthen their relations *vis-à-vis* the neighbouring Manghyt sovereigns and Karakalpak and Kalmyk tribes but also actively participated in trade relations with Bashkiria and Siberia. They also maintained their sphere of control *vis-à-vis* the Ufa administration of the imperial Russian state.[13]

There is also an attempt to restore the egalitarian and democratic character of the Kazakh nomadic organization formative phases, describing special features of the medieval Kazakh khanate in order to relieve it from the stigma of being a corrosive feudal state. Till 1628, the Kazakh Khans not only reformed their political apparatus and judicial system with adequate support from the three *zhuzes* but established themselves as representatives of an amalgam of authorities of the highest order (referred to by the metaphor *aq suiek* or 'white bone'). The sultan-chingizids or the *tora* (claiming descent from Chingiz Khan) as well as the *khoja* (of Arab origin and claiming descent from Prophet Muhammad) represented the aristocratic order while the rest of the population (with the metaphoric notion *qara suiek* or 'black bone') were required to perform an array of administrative, judicial and military functions. Common ancestry bound these two strata together and safeguarding the Kazakh state was their joint responsibility while a Council of Elders was to advise the sultans in decision-making. Quite clearly, it was 'steppe democracy' that got a fresh lease of life in the new evaluation of Kazakh history.[14]

Another feature of this image restoration is movements by Kazakh families that occurred not simply because the Kazakh herders were lured by newer pastures or lands for grazing but because they were driven to interact with the economically and militarily more powerful groups. Another reason for this flocked movement could be the growth of herds forcing certain sections of the pastoral community to move to other places. Nomad movements were determined by clan affiliations and studies have concentrated on shifting allegiances after the Nogai-Uzbek-Kazakh union dissolved in the late fifteenth and early sixteenth centuries.[15] So, within Kazakh nomadism there were tendencies of fission as well as fusion. The long-range perspective of Kazakh political tradition tends to bring together all these components and internal dissensions leading to political desertions, 'property-sharing' (i.e. movable as in the case of land and immovable as in the case of livestock), herd composition, Kazakh legal structure outlined by the *zheti zhargy* (seven codes) sanctioned by Khan Tauke's regime have been discussed within this framework. The colonial dispensation of the nineteenth century transformed that set-up—

the primacy of the *zhuz* faded and there was diffusion of power among tribal leaders who represented the *volosts* and *auls*. The domain of the Kazakh customary law or *adat* was reconstituted and the *biys* became the principal adjudicators of disputes, who enforced judgements like *barymta* (taking away of livestock). Another significant feature is the spiritual behaviour among the Kazakhs. Literature on the Kazakhs' adherence to certain Islamic practices, the Islamic transformation on the Kazakh steppe in the eighteenth century and interactions leading to the formation of Muslim communities under the auspices of spiritual assemblies and the dissemination of Tatar education among wealthy Kazakh nomad families increased.[16] The 'world-view' of *tengrism* (from 'tengri' meaning sky, hence, sky worship) which was popular among the Kazakh nomads, its monotheistic concept of the *Blue Sky*, of a single god governing the whole world and the intertwining of shamanist traditions and *tengrism* are yet to be comprehensively studied. However, there seems to be growing recognition of *tengrism* as the unifier and a political tradition in the steppe that calls for the unity of the steppe people under a clan leader. Images of a mighty Kazakh khanate with illustrious names as Kasym Khan, Tauke Khan and Ablai Khan who aspired to unite all tribal groups under the single military slogan *Uran-Alash!* that was echoed by the people's government in 1918 to muster support for the Alash Orda movement have assumed prominence.[17]

TRANSFORMATION OF THE STEPPE: SOVIET AND POST-SOVIET STUDIES

The restoration of the steppe profile has been seriously attempted by studies that have referred to the Kazakhs' colonial past. Recounting historical milestones in the 300-year power relationship between the Russians and the Kazakhs beginning from the sixtgeenth century, studies have indicated (a) the Golden Horde disintegration and (b) the rejuvenation of horde status by the Middle Horde. The Middle Horde sultans' exercise of power *vis-à-vis* their competitors is a fact. The indeterminate nature of relations (mostly diplomatic exchanges) were replaced by concrete trade negotiations in the eighteenth century and which finally enticed the Middle Horde Kazakh sultans in the nineteenth century to be partisans of a colonial apparatus. The evolution of Russo-Kazakh relations from infrequent trade and diplomatic exchanges to concrete negotiations with the Lesser Horde and the Middle Horde Khans has been interpreted in various ways. Abul Khair's tactful manouvering of Russian support in the Bashkir territory is viewed as a repositioning of the Lesser Horde Khans *vis-à-vis* Dzhungar threat in the east. Kazakh 'allegiance' and 'submission' is sometimes grossly overstated because Abul Khair apparently was intent on enhancing his own authority at the expense of the Russians who were extremely encouraged by the consolidation of their position in Bashkiria along the Ural River. Disputes over the land question came into sharp focus during Russia's dealings with the Lesser and Middle Hordes and the subsequent delineation of territories which according to Steven Sabol's review of Kazakh responses to Russian colonization, 'not only obstructed nomadic movement but cut across historic emblems of identity such as *zhuz*, which were connected to genealogy and territory. The Kazaks [Kazakhs] were affected specifically by the Regulations on Siberian Kirghiz and the *Kishi zhuz* Kazaks as "Orenburg Kirgiz".'[18] In fact, land appears to be the key element that reconfigured not only Kazakhs' relations with the Russians but also Kazakhs' strenuous relations with Kokand. The ways in which relationships altered during the colonial period have been treated differently by the Soviet and post-Soviet historians. Some of their perspectives will be studied in this section.

Soviet historians portrayed the Kazakhs as integral to the Russian set-up and hence a distinctive Kazakh framework is entirely missing from Soviet representations of history. An exception was the early Soviet writer M. Viatkin who belonged to Soviet Union's first generation of historians and inspired by the 'fatherland's victory' in 1941 was concerned about writing about the community of nationalities and their role in the reconstitution of the fatherland. Russo-Kazakh relations was an obvious choice and Viatkin pointed to 'generational contacts' that evolved ever since St. Petersburg's administrative corpus represented by local Kazakhs like Chokan Valikhanov became actively interested in the steppe and its intertwined histories. Mukhtar Auezov was the next generation Soviet Kazakh writer whose critique of the feudal *biys* and reflections on the germination of enlightenment ideas within younger generations of the steppe lords were applauded by his Soviet patrons. Auezov's favourite character was Abai Kunanbayev, the Kazakh poet who despite his upbringing in a feudal family repudiated hegemonic control of the feudal lords. Auezov was spiritually inspired by Abai Kunanbaev because he represented a contrast to his authoritative surroundings. Auezov, Abai's voice, became a rehabilitated writer of Khrushchev's generation. Soviet musings about Auezov's literary contributions reflected their respect for a writer who echoed Abai's thoughts that were coloured by sentimentality and emotion. The emotion was about Kazakh village life powered by patriarchy. Auezov's prose had a tragic content, reflecting on the undying character of political tradition in the Kazakh steppe. The enlighteners' penchant for love was a different domain—it was different from the feudal lords' harsh practices.

The duality of steppe life, a late nineteenth century steppe dispensation, was a subject that was also treated by Abai's contemporaries in Central Asia and Transcaucasia, especially Sadridin Aini and Shirvanzade. Auezov's three-volume fictional composition on the life of Abai reflected on his life and times. The daring son of Kunanbai lived in a village called Esembai that resonated with the songs of the wandering minstrels and bards (*baksi*). Auezov recreated the world of Abai and reflected on its contrasting features—the cruelty of the *biys*, the prestige of the Golden Horde preserved by steppe patriarchal traditions and authoritarian gestures of the patriarchs of the tribal village and the role of assemblages in everyday life, periodic movements of the Kazakh nomads to their summer and winter pastures on the one hand and the mood of dissent among the younger generations who learnt to live amidst fears of pillage and robbery by arbitrary gang leaders. The disorder that spread as rich Khans were looted and mobbed by robbers in the open space overlapping the Semipalatinsk *uezd* that was governed by the Tsar's administrators was sketched by Auezov in his classic composition *Abai*. The youth collaborated with Russian generals who supervised the villages in their jurisdiction. There was a blossoming of new ideas as Russian poetry reached the villages and touched the hearts of enlightened Kazakhs like Abai Kunanbayev. In Auezov's verse, we get an impression of the Kazakhs' Russian past and how the advent of the Russians rehabilitated the Kazakh mind. Auezov was the new voice of the nineteenth-century enlighteners Chokan Valikhanov and Abay Kunanbaev who consistently placed hopes on the Kazakhs' Russian destiny.[19]

In post-Soviet literature, the attention shifts to Kazakh activism of the nineteenth century. Historians have portrayed the Kazakh nomads not as recipients of the Russian 'order' but as a belligerent force that became unmanageable, specially when it combined with other regional forces. In this case, the Kazakh Khans' manipulation of steppe sentiments in the other khanates (Kokand khanate) became a reference point for a study of the intricate web of tribal relationships. The Kazakhs also became collaborators of the imperial steppe administration—a perspective with added emphasis on the intricacies of colonial management. The ways in which an entire line of military fortresses from Orenburg to Omsk was managed by imperial administrators and military governors serving Russian ministries of war and internal affairs tends to be interlinked to the study of Kazakh activism. The spectacle of colonial administration, the methods of colonial governance, the presence of Russian peasant settlements in Kazakh pasturelands that had a corrosive effect on Kazakh economy and disrupted the mechanism of internal control by the Khans are intrinsic to such discussions about Kazakh history. The trajectory of a colonial other, i.e. the belligerent force that was estranged from an enlightened Kazakh spectrum, sets the tone of a set of writings that represents the critique of imperial governance and imperial motivations in the steppe. Another set of writings is more concerned with the regenerative aspect of the Kazakhs and concentrates on the didactic reformist literature of Kazakhstan as in the rest of Central Asia. The first set of writings is mostly of an interpretative nature and there is an attempt to reflect on 'institutional memory' as a way of understanding the spontaneous character of Kazakh rebellions.[20] The Kazakh rebelliousness was the *outcome* of colonial policies of the nineteenth century. The colonial hangover of the Kazakhs was exclusively related to what the Kazakhs experienced or encountered *after* the colonial makeover. Kenesary Kasymov's revolt (1837-47) vaguely described as anti-imperial resistance, was associated with Kazakhs' reassertion of land rights. Now, this was not a unique venture in terms of Kazakh steppe discipline because throughout the eighteenth century, Kasymov's predecessors Abul Khair and Emelian Pugachev had tried to *cross* the military line of the Cossacks (the Ishim Line for instance) and migrate unhindered by any authority. Stringent regulations pertaining to the delineation of Kazakh confederated structures (*auls* and *yurts* being reintegrated into *volosts*) were also not acceptable in Kazakh terms.

Kenesary's revolt was primarily the outcome of disaffection regarding confiscation of land by the Russians. Analysts are probably right when they certify it as a Kazakh attempt to reassert the authority of the Khan. The Russian fortifications on Kazakh migratory routes were a direct threat to Kazakh traditional nomadic movements and both Abul Khair and Pugachev had set the trend of resistance in a steppe locale. Here was the issue of sentiment as the Kazakhs' mobility was hampered by the Russian encroachments. But there was an internal reason too. Kenesary's rival, the Zhappas clan joined the Russian Siberian detachment which could have insulted the Khan and stopped him from punishing his rivals with punitive action (*barymta*). Kenesary was hardly a mobilizer in the truest sense of the term because not every clan supported him. The Kazakhs had very feeble support of the Kokand khanate, their only steppe neighbour. Khiva was suppressed by the Russians very easily. Therefore, tenuous relationships and awkward friendships sealed the fate of Kenesary's revolt. To idealize the revolt as the first national-liberation movement is a prejudiced approach. More appropriate is the argument that it was an attempt to assert khanship and the revolt was a move to revive the legacy of control that was fading away in the context of the new Tsarist dispensation, especially with the construction of the Cossack military line along river Ural and also the Tsarist statutes that were targeting the land of the Kazakhs. A series of 'regulations' between 1868-91 that readjusted Kazakh settings and placed Kazakh grazing lands under different directorates of imperial control, namely (a) governor-generalship of Turkestan, (b) governor-generalship of Orynbor, (c) governor-generalship of western Siberia and (d) steppe governor-generalship centred in Omsk, may have caused a great deal of anxiety.

This leads us to other interesting aspects about Kazakh history and the Kazakhs' relations with the Russians in a less turbulent period, i.e. sixteenth-eighteenth centuries which were far more complicated and were dependent on myriad links that evolved since Empress Catherine's tolerant policy towards the nomads. 'Integrationist moves' began during the reign of Catherine the Great, especially in the 1730s when there was an attempt to manage the belligerent *biys* and *sultans* in order to safeguard the trade with Bukhara that passed through the steppe once the traditional caravan routes through Astrakhan and Kazan were cut-off. The necessity to safeguard trading interests brought the Russian *voevody* (military governor) into direct contact with Kazakh nomad chieftains like Abul Khair in the seventeenth century. So, the Kazakh steppe was like a pathway of trade in the sixteenth-eighteenth centuries, with no direct relations with the Russian authorities. Loose contacts were maintained but that too through envoy dispatches—an important feature of the findings and 'ethnographic enquiries' of St. Petersburg's IRGO specialists like Valikhanov who were sent on imperial missions in the nineteenth century, very often in the guise of merchants, to report on the possibilities of renewing such contacts after periodic disruptions that took place due to intermittent inter-tribal dissensions among the Nogais, Oirats and the Kazakhs or due to spurts of rebellion initiated by adversaries like Iset Kotybarov, Srym Batyr and Abul Khair who were hardly concerned with Russian protectionism. The oaths of loyalty and allegiance of the chieftains were very superficial and the conditions of fealty indicate the inner workings of Kazakh tribal society.

Against this backdrop of Kazakh activism one needs to assess the multiple versions about Kazakh steppe history. In reappraisals of steppe history, historians highlighted the steppe not only as a scene of transformation affected by military rule and colonization and waves of migration but also as an arena where nomads had their own conditions and created difficulties for the colonial regime. The responsibility of administering the nomadic people was not easy and it appeares that it was in connection with the assumption of grazing lands and the relinquishing of herding rights by the Kazakhs that the colonial government got into a far more difficult situation than was imagined. Colonization was clearly a chaotic affair that was managed haphazardly by administrators that put many Kazakhs at risk for survival.[21] The imposition of colonial administration (through reorganization of the Lesser Horde, expulsion of the Middle Horde and military subjugation of the Golden Horde) consolidated Russian position *vis-à-vis* the Kazakhs and it was the land question and the debate over the farming abilities of the Kazakhs that gave the Russians a stronger edge. The Turkestan and Steppe statutes abided by the principle of land ownership for the Kazakhs but were more sympathetic to land usage by the Russians. With the incorporation of Semirechie and Syr Darya *oblasts* within Steppe administration, the Russian and Ukrainian settlers got an advantage particularly after the imperial decrees of 1891 and 1893 that gave them total control of renting lands on which they settled almost impromptu. In 1896, a decree gave them control over Kazakh homesteads and with that the dispossession of Kazakh nomads of the Golden Horde was complete.

It was alleged that the Russian land policy practically destroyed Kazakh economy. Negative perceptions prevailed over campaign programmes, especially those related to resettlement and sedentarization of the Kazakh nomads. By the 1890s, land of the northern Kazakhs who practised limited agriculture came under intense pressure due to the impact of peasant colonization in west Siberia and the Kazakh steppe.[22] Peasant resettlement in the steppe had far-reaching effects. The Resettlement Act of 1889 and the Steppe Code of 1891 permitted the Slavic peasants to migrate and settle on Kazakh lands without paying much attention to the Kazakh migratory routes. The increased pace of colonization disrupted traditional migratory routes and impoverished many Kazakhs unable to adapt to the new economic conditions. The concept of individual ownership of land further eroded their socio-political structure. The Russians imposed a new economic structure in which only the wealthy Kazakhs were willing to cooperate. Therefore, social fragmentation in frontier societies, already set in motion by land problems among agricultural communities in the steppe, increased due to colonization and peasant resettlement. Western scholars have scathingly criticized the land settlement policy of the Tsarist authorities. Martha Brill Olcott's suggestion that it brought an end to Kazakh nomadism is somewhat exaggerated[23] though Peter Rottier has pinpointed the problem about 'excess lands' of the nomads (which virtually did not exist in the strict nomadic sense) in Akmolinsk *oblast.* In his opinion, land was omnipresent in the Kazakh psyche and the Tsarist moves resulted in shrinkage of pastures for livestock that actually triggered the movement.[24] It was alleged that the Kazakhs were assigned poor quality lands on the basis of the settlement norms while the best lands were reserved for Russian settlers. Count Pahlen, the officer surveying such moves of the colonization department, criticized this and other abuses of the colonial policies. The 'sedentarization' of the Kazakhs became a serious matter and was questioned by the Kazakh intellectuals of the early twentieth century. Scholars are, however, not unanimous about the issue of appropriation of lands by the colonial regime. Their argument is that the pastoral lands of the Kazakhs had already started to erode long before the programme of resettlement. However, the fact remains that the steppe emerged as a settler colony and the Russian peasants and Cossacks fuelled the demographic colonization of the Kazakh steppe. The Cossacks, as a privileged military caste, were the agents of colonization and Russification. The others were political convicts and exiles who were sent to the steppe for hard labour and became unwitting agents of colonization. Sometimes old Believers, non-Orthodox Christians also fled to distant lands in the steppe, in north Kazakhstan and close to Siberia, to escape the rigidity of Orthodox norms.

Only the new settlers felt the advantages of colonial administration. Tsarist authorities tried to cope with pressure on land through counter-measures and modifications, namely reclamation of swampland and drainage expeditions in and around Moscow and St. Petersburg. The impact of such drainage operations was felt in the wide marshes of western Siberia and along the Trans-Siberian Railway. The new settlements surrounding the entire railway tract were the 'home environment' of the Russian peasant settlers—as argued by Willard Sunderland in his engrossing study of Russian peasant pioneering in the newly colonized and the newly reclaimed lands in the Russian hinterland.[25] The encouragement and incentives (tax exemptions) provided by the authorities to the 'pioneers' in order to settle and establish new villages in the south inspired numerous peasant settlers and farmers to migrate from Muscovy and settle in and around the Irtysh River. The lure of 'attractive places' in the east and the excitement of crossing the Volga and entering Siberia or scouting the hilly hinterlands up to Vladivostok were evident in the settlers' letters to their relatives in Russia. Land was a major concern in their accounts and there was an overriding expectation of finding good land. Also, the places the settlers had moved to seemed to have abundant resources—from vegetables to fruits, berries and timber. In settlers' accounts, there is a clear line of distinction between Russia on the other side of the Urals that was full of hardship compared to the settlers' new home on the frontier where life was better. The railroad links with Omsk and Orenburg and Tashkent offered better prospects for connectivity with the Russian market compared to Syr Darya and Semirechie oblasts.

The Russians' defence settlements were also a feature of the transformation that had taken place in the south of Moscow and Russia's steppe frontier in the colonial period. A Siberian defence line across the west Siberian plain up to the Altai foothills and about 4,000 km in length was suitable to safeguard west Siberia from the wrath of the native princes (Dzhungars) and native horsemen (Kalmyks, Kazakhs, Bashkirs) in the south. The frontier defense system of the Russians was very sophisticated and technologically advanced and could combat the horse riders of the steppe during the seventeenth-nineteenth centuries. The *zaseki* (fortified lines) in the forest steppe region of southern Russia, *voevoda* (line of forts linked to each other by sentinel service) along Tobol, Irtysh, Yenisei and Ob rivers, *stanitsy* (Cossack settlements) were and distinguishing features of the 4,000 km-stretch of the Slavic military frontier that extended from the Caspian shores and across the west Siberian plain along the Irtysh and along the foothills of the Altai up to the Kazakh grasslands. This entire region (i.e. from Urals to the Irtysh and south to the Kazakh) comprising peasant settlers, craftsmen and iron smelters was protected by a line of forts and defence lines and was safe from the attacks of the Kazakhs from the south (because the latter were virtually cut-off). They were also protected by Siberian Cossacks and servitors from various Siberian towns and indentured people from neighbouring communities. There were collaborators like the service Tatars (*sluzhilye Tatary*) in Tobolsk and Tyumen who fought on behalf of the Russian armies and inflicted final defeat on Kuchum Khan in the Baraba steppe in 1598. Merchant adventurers and Cossack conquistadors were considered to be the first group of people to reach the steppe frontier. Gradually, as private initiatives had the full backing of the Muscovite state, the region drew in Russian fur-trappers and traders, who were later accompanied by *sluzhilye lyudi* and *voennosluzhilye lyudi* (administrative and military personnel) who were engaged in agriculture and a variety of trades and crafts. Very soon, there was a surge of other economic activities related to the extraction of gold, silver, lead, iron, copper and mica. Soviet historians are of the opinion that *voennosluzhilye lyudi* comprised the largest section of Russian settlers in the Siberian plains, as in any other fortress settlements of Central Asia.[26] Many other writers share this view and have emphasized on the lead role played by fortress towns in the Russian expansion towards the north and the east.[27] Their writings focus not on the colonization process *per se*, but on the agents of change, especially the settler communities who were protected by Russian defence lines that extended up to the Baraba wooded steppe.

KAZAKH CONSCIENCE

The social milieu and moral obligations of a conscientious intelligentsia received a great deal of attention in discussions about the 'transformation' of a Kazakh space that was primarily a Golden Horde territory and a Middle Horde sphere of control. A majority of writings reflected on sedentarization and its lopsided effect on the Kazakh economy.[28] Land became a persistent issue of debate in the Russian Dumas of the early twentieth century. The inception of this subject in intellectual discourse has also been indicated in studies about the exclusive dynamic role of the steppe intelligentsia and the restructuring of imperial relationships. This subject of community interaction has lately developed as a field of specialization in the West as scholars like Allen Frank and Steven Sabol have started sharing the views of their Japanese counterparts Uyama Tomohiko and Naganawa Norihiro. Their works have revoked earlier assumptions about 'hostile relations' in the imperial fabric. According to Tomohiko, sedentarization resulted in 'a strategic alliance between Kazakh intellectuals and Russian administrators'.[29] In his opinion, the colonial environment offered a unique opportunity to Kazakh intellectuals to express themselves as a social stratum with a feeling of responsibility. The Kazakh intellectuals expressed their views through their interactive newspaper *Dala Walayatining Gazeti* (1882-1902) that was published by the governor-generalate of the steppe. The officially stated aims of the newspaper were to make the Kazakh people aware of the instructions of the Russian authorities that were related to the administering of the Kazakh steppe. Information about the economic life of the inhabitants (stock breeding, barter, farming methods, etc.) and spiritual life (traditions, legends, folk tales, democratic traditions) was disseminated. The editorials of the newspaper indicated that it was an interactive medium for transmitting official views of the governor-generalate and a forum for representing Russian and Kazakh views. The news were mainly local, based on the governor-general's orders, his tours of inspection, his meetings with local Kazakh administrators in Torghay, Uralsk, and Syr Darya oblasts. Such reports indicate the empire's network with its localities. Omsk, the centre of the governor-generalate, was the connecting link with local culture. The organization of an exhibition on Kazakh cuisine, nomadic dwellings and commodity display in Omsk in 1891, the arrival of the first train on the Siberian Railroad in Omsk in 1894 were features of this intense exhibitionism of imperial patronage. Reports on the Tsar's entourage, royal events (e.g. Crown Prince Nikolai's wedding), protectionist measures (e.g. circular about petitions) indicated the Kazakhs' loyalty towards the authorities. Articles from *Turkestan Vilayetining Gazeti* were reproduced to indicate the regional contact. The 'world-view' of the newspaper connoted the Russian Muslims, Chinese Muslims, Indian Muslims and Muslims of the Ottoman Empire. The superficiality of the Russian reforms at the local level was also pointed out. For example, the *volost* officials did only selective rounds for the collection of taxes. Local people were equally inefficient in the handling of administration. Local judicial practices and the malfunctioning of the *bis'* courts were highlighted. By pointing to these weaknesses in the administrative apparatus, the newspaper tried to report on the real, not the abstract. Therefore, a whole range of subjects were covered—education (referring to models of Tatar education, Russian education, institutions of education, partnership between educated men who professed the need to educate Kazakh people), sedentarization and agriculture, marriage and status of women. There was a constant attempt to project on opinions of progress so that the Kazakhs could learn to be mature and introspective. The limitation of this newspaper was that it failed to report on non-Muslim regions of Russia and hence was unable to reach out to all communities. Moreover, it reflected transcendental awareness about reformism—an aspect that hardly touched the entire spectrum of Kazakh society. Evidently, the critique of Kazakh tribal norms and authoritarian behaviour was completely dissociated from the rubric of paternalism and tribal hegemony, a fact that has been touched upon by Mukhtar Auezov in his recreated life story of Abay Kunanbaev.

The reformist phenomenon was all-pervasive and this aspect has been analysed by Tomohiko. The intellectual leaders were not merely moral guardians of their people but also gained prominence as activists who were involved in the day-to-day proceedings of the Alash programme for autonomy that was linked with a Turkistani agenda of the Kokand Autonomous government or the *oblastniki's* agenda in Siberia. In presenting a biographical sketch of the intellectuals, Tomohiko argues that there was a correlation between the varied geographical backgrounds of the individuals.[30] Interaction between these individuals and the Russian establishment was possible because most of them though belonging to a nomadic environment, experienced the benefits of an educated environment in Omsk, Orenburg, Semipalatinsk, Kazan and St. Petersburg. The intellectuals who studied in small towns were reared in big influential families and therefore had the privilege of travelling to big cities that gave them an opportunity of comparing 'spaces'—the domain of convention and the domain of liberalism and change. What they encountered in the new space was articulated through their ideas and programmes. Tomohiko's analysis of the intellectual careers of prominent Kazakh educationists and enlighteners highlights the intellectual ferment in the Middle Horde enclaves of Qostanai and Torghai in the 1850s that was articulated in the autonomy programme of the Alash party in the 1920s. According to Tomohiko therefore, there was a Kazakh intellectual reckoning of Russian, nomadic and Islamic contexts.

Tomohiko's views about a collaborative atmosphere are examined by other scholars too. In their retrospective analysis of the Kazakh intelligentsia, they have tried to re-invent its role not as an activist generation experimenting with the fuzzy ideals of national-liberation movement or federalism but as a caucus of enlighteners who morally guided their people. The intellectuals echoed ideas of Russian slavophilism as much as they highlighted their sensitivities about a nomadic heritage. The euphoria about Kazakh national consciousness tends to revolve around discussions about self-examination of the Kazakh intelligentsia. Kazakhness, according to the Kazakh intelligentsia, meant not disorganized response, but unity in action and thought, the dialectics of which have also been indicated.[31] The centre of attention is independent thinking that flourished in Omsk and other parts of northern and western Kazakhstan, the aristocratic background and career-profile of ideologues and activists who were trained by the Russian government as educators or service personnel and worked within the tsarist apparatus. There are also reflections about an earlier generation of conscientious Kazakhs who because of a Russian environment in Omsk where they were trained as military officers, were motivated to meet the challenges of a naturally Kazakh environment. The 'unusual partnership' between the Ministry of Education represented by N.I. Ilminskii and the schools imparting exclusive Kazakh education also produced a generation of students who were receptive to the instructions of their masters.[32] It is this relationship of accommodation between Russia and her imperial subjects that is the major theme of the discourse about integrative mechanisms in the educational centres. The Kazakh intellectual sphere opens with the life and times of the first modern Kazakh intellectual, Chokan Valikhanovich Valikhanov (Shoqan Walikhanov in Kazakh, 1835-65). He was a scholar-enlightener whose family background and military training (in the cadet corps of Omsk) brought him into close contact with notable orientalists like G.N. Potanin, outstanding Russian novelists like Dostoevsky (who encouraged him to write about the Kazakh people and interpret the steppe for Russia) and military personnel of the Siberian Line Cossack army that served the western Siberian governor-generalate which was responsible for organizing scientific expeditions to regions that were opening up as sensitive hotspots of Chinese or eastern Turkestan. In the course of a brief life span he rose to prominence from a khanate repository[33] to the highest echelons of the Russian scholarly community. In the words of his biographer Kermit McKenzie, Valikhanov believed that Russia was the most important conveyor of education and progress. Like Ibrahim Altynsaryn and Abay Kunanbaev, Valikhanov was an unwavering advocate of friendship between the Russian and Kazakh people. Valikhanov's life illuminates the following themes of historical importance: (a) interaction between nomadic and sedentary lifestyles, classical Islamic learning and Russian education; (b) the birth of a colonial intelligentsia and its strategic alliance with imperial apparatus; (c) imperial institutions like Imperatorskovo Geograficheskovo Obshchestva (IRGO) which patronized local intellectuals and sent them on imperial missions; (d) nineteenth-century Anglo-Russian-Chinese rivalry for ascendancy in Inner Asia which emerged as the fulcrum of steppe politics since the eighteenth century. Imperial China's control over eastern Turkestan and the replacement of aggression by collaboration represented the new political reality in the steppe that was no longer shaped by the authority of masters like Ablai Khan. McKenzie points out, 'the changing posture toward Russia as manifested successively by Ablai, Vali, Chingis (Valikhanov's father) and Chokan reveals what happened in one branch of the Kazakh aristocracy'.[34]

Valikhanov's training in Omsk was a unique experience for this aristocrat-son who soon became a close companion of the veteran Cossack radical thinker Georgi Potanin. Despite the age difference, Potanin respected young Valikhanov as 'an interesting subject' with a passionate interest in Kazakh folklore. Like European intellectuals of the early nineteenth century, prominent sections of the Kazakh elite became interested in a phenomenon of what is called 'the discovery of the people'. The paternalistic influence of the intellectuals, their indulgence in folk tales, folk songs, popular festivals and various genres of folk culture that made them the 'brothers' of the ordinary people is an aspect of Kazakh nation-building, according to Uyama Tomohiko.[35] Omsk was a major centre of dissemination of literature on the steppe territory. The place was a revelation as a great repository of Russian literary figures and activist groups like the Decembrists. In Omsk, Valikhanov utilized the archives of the Siberian administration and deepened his knowledge about the farthest outposts of Central Asia in the east. His knowledge of the Chagatai language (spoken by Turkic business families) helped him in his imperial mission to eastern Turkestan in the 1850s where he travelled as a Marghelani merchant. Valikhanov became the illustrious explorer in service of the frontier administration of the Tsarist government in western Siberia and the suburbs of Omsk. Valikhanov's name as permanent member of the IRGO was recommended strongly by Semenov Tyan Shanskii, another frontier explorer. Valikhanov's field surveys in the Kyrgyz country and the region around Issyk Kul in 1856 and during the Kashgar mission of 1858-9 turned the spotlight on him as an intelligence agent who navigated Dzhungaria and little-known Chinese provinces and whose reports were published by the Russian Geographical Society. Valikhanov's impressions about Chinese strongholds in eastern Turkestan were treated as valuable information by his superiors in Omsk. The master explorer was a prolific writer of almost every aspect of steppe life and culture. He attained celebrity status at the young age of 30 years. In St. Petersburg, he prepared reports for the Asiatic Department and maps for the War Ministry, presented eloquent talks at the Geographical Society and engaged himself in university activities in St. Petersburg. Towards the end of his life, Valikhanov became harshly critical about illiteracy among the nomads, the hostility of the nobility and above all the practitioners of Muslim faith who were incapable of reforms. He suggested that reforms for his people could be brought to effect by the Russian administration on the basis of the advice of the Kazakh intellectuals. Neither the rich Kazakhs, nor the Tatar beneficiaries could bring about reforms on their own. This aversion towards Tatar activism was reflected in many other thinkers of the nineteenth century and is a vindication of the variety of responses towards cultural revivalism.[36]

The prevention of Tatarization was the basic aim of most of the intellectual reformers associated with the publishing world dominated by newspapers and journals like *Dala Walayitining Gazeti* and *Ai Qap*. Russian education, for all intellectuals, was an instrument to awaken the people. Valikhanov and Altynsaryn were the beginners and worked in their respective fields to raise the level of consciousness among the Kazakh people. Abai Kunanbaev's role in popularizing Russian classical texts in the Semipalatinsk province through prose and poetry is the subject matter of Mukhtar Auezov's three-part literary novel *Abai Zholy* (*The Path of Abai*). Abai's works were devoted to the Kazakh youth 'with a reasonable and clear mind' and inspired Kazakh activists of the early twentieth century. Like Valikhanov, he urged the Kazakhs to educate themselves through the knowledge of Russian which 'acts a shield, as a pillar for people'. The generation that succeeded Abai echoed his words and followed the activist programme of the Decembrists and the Narodniks who were exiled to the steppe territory. To this generation belonged Alikhan Bukeikhanov (1866-1937) and Mir Yaqub Dulatov (1885-1935) whose passion to serve the people appealed to several members of the Alash Orda movement. The zeal is explicit in Dulatov's book *Oyan, Qazak* (Awake, Qazaq!).

Language was a pivotal issue in the reformist literature that was published during this time and had huge emotional appeal among the Alash Orda activists who had imbibed the ideas of the 1905 revolution. The search for temporary allies continued till the provisional government took charge of affairs after the February Revolution in 1917. This in fact indicates the wariness among Kazakh intellectuals and their dilemma about what is to be done. In fact, the deliberations of the congresses and conferences of the early twentieth century indicate that the intelligentsia encountered enormous difficulties in order to unify politically. While there was general agreement among the intelligentsia on the causes behind the Kazakhs' social and economic plight, solutions were disputed. But this failure about a political consensus in no way indicates the absence of a wider shared perception of the world around them. So, the unity that the intellectuals represented was a psychological one. Disagreements that erupted between the Western-oriented intellectuals with *Ai Qap* as their principal mouthpiece and the nationalists who were traditionalists and had *Kazak* as their principal publication did not affect the intellectuals psychologically. Nor did it affect their minds in their long journey as ideologues who matured into activists.

The years 1905-17 has been represented as a period of hectic political activity among the Kazakhs.[37] In studies of movements for national liberation, petitions and demands that were put forward by Kazakh intellectuals to protest against government interference regarding the role of Islamic law courts have been re-examined closely. There were further demands for the return of all lands seized from the Kazakhs (and given to Russian peasants) and protection had to be rendered in case of further seizures. The basic motivation was the democratic movement of the Russian liberals and the intellectuals established contacts with the Russian Constitutional Democratic Party. Demands about Kazakh-language religious instructions and increasing the influence of the local Muslim clergy were also raised. According to Dina Amanzhalova, an expert of the autonomy movements of Central Asia and Siberia in the twentieth century, these petitions reflected the federal alternatives of the Russian state as well as its successor Soviet state.[38] The creation of the *muftiat* in the steppe region was the first indication of the intellectuals' victory, though it is considered to be the logical culmination of Catherine II's policy of 'pragmatic flexibility'.[39] After 1905, the law became more flexible on 'religious toleration'. Drawing on these details, liberal enthusiasts have depicted the milieu of collaboration between a self-aware Kazakh elite, local Muslim communities and a literate clergy. The Kazakh intellectuals while arguing their cases in the First and Second Dumas also represented the Islamic world-view. In other words, there was euphoric appeal about enlightenment and the intellectuals made relentless efforts through their newspapers to transmit the knowledge of enlightenment.

After the February Revolution, the mood changed and the euphoria was about political and spiritual freedom. The milestones during this phase were association with the Constitutional Democrats (Kadets) and the Muslim faction raising petitions, especially about land question (in contrast to the zeal for curricular education at an earlier phase) and local court performances given the movement a degree of political status—a subject that has been treated in the new literature about Alash Orda activism in the steppe.

In a separate treatment about what each of these petitions represented, scholars have dealt not only with the aspect of land reform but also with the extent to which these reforms could be implemented. In fact, once the intellectuals got a political platform, they started questioning the 'reach' of freedom. The Kazakh population was warned against unethical interpretations of freedom—e.g. plundering caravans, exercising *barymta* (positive action like taking away of livestock), cutting trees without permission or mob-attacks on storehouses (as had happened in Vernyi/Almata in the aftermath of the February Revolution). So, what began as Kazakh social concerns metamorphosed into issues of political concern and during the war years the Kazakh intellectuals like Bukeikhanov never missed an opportunity to debate on issues that were critical to the nomadic set-up. The support of the Alash programme by the Kadets and the Muslim caucus, the wide circulation of the intellectual newspapers *Serke*, *Qazaqstan* and *Alash* during 1905-17, the popularization of Kazakh tradition in *Ai Qap* gave new meaning to the political role of Kazakh intellectuals. The influence of the lobbying groups among the intellectuals in the pre-1917 phase has inspired different levels of debates regarding the kind of alternatives the intellectuals represented. The psychological motivation was always present and this attributes to an alternative discourse about liberation. The desire to liberate the mind has made the Kazakh intelligentsia a prime focus of study. Scholars who have reviewed Kazakh intellectualism feel that their potential as political activists was limited.

The intellectuals faced a serious test when a tsarist *ukase* (decree) issued conscription of nomads in 1916. The issue became an occasion for Kazakh resistance throughout Turkestan and the steppe. There were sporadic outbursts of revolt and the rebels resorted to haphazard actions like reinstating khans who hardly belonged to the Chingizid lineage or whimsically acting as leaders of the Arghyn tribe that tried to form a quasi-state. Sometimes, sudden outbursts took place between Islamic contingents of the rebels and their Russian peasants. Sometimes, the *mullahs* as guardians of tradition were resistant to the rebels in Kazakhstan. Due to such disparate tendencies, there have been attempts to review the 1916 revolt with which the intellectuals could not get involved. The subject of Kazakh resistance hardly inspired the enthusiastic supporters of national liberation who pinned hopes on the alternatives that were put forth by the intellectuals who posed as mediators and whose guidance was not accepted by the leaders of a spontaneous uprising. The 1916 revolt alienated the intellectuals to a certain extent and was eventually shunned by the Soviet Kazakh official circles. From the early years of the Soviet period, it is only star personalities like Valikhanov who have been elevated to the status of a cult figure. In post-Soviet writings about leaders and leadership programmes, the role of the intelligentsia has found new meaning.

KAZAKH RELIGIOSITY

Collaboration with Muslim religious institutions is another area of research on Kazakhstan. Naganawa Norihiro describes the interrelationships between the state and the community that led to the formation of a regional Muslim identity centering Orenburg. Norihiro's candid assertions about the interactions between the Muslims' daily life and imperial governance, especially after the establishment of the Mohammedan Spiritual Assembly in Orenburg in 1905,[40] is one way of assessing a Muslim institutional legacy. Another group of scholars, also belonging to the revivalist school, point out that Russian 'transformation' of the steppe is not the complete story—it is not the essence of the Kazakhs' imperial past. Allen Frank's version of an Islamic transformation is related to the prominence of Kazakh hagiolatry, Kazakh customary law among the southern and western regions of Kazakhstan and the interaction of these regions with the Central Asiatic Islamic establishments. There was also a dominant Islamic discourse about education at the rural level, a point stressed in Frank's study of Islamic teaching.[41] Frank extended his analysis to the Muslim institutional sphere, the active educational role of Volga-Tatar communities, which also facilitated the development of national identities in the twentieth century. The dynamic local Islamic setting in the steppe and the network of religious personnel who acted independently of the spiritual assembly and a web of pastoral nomadic activities of the Bashkirs, Inner Horde Kazakhs (who belonged to the Lesser Horde or Junior Horde) and the Ural Cossacks (comprising of the Russians, Kalmyks and the Tatars) is a revelation of the local spiritual dimension irrespective of the overall patronage of the Muslim assemblies. The sacred geography of a Muslim community disseminated by local texts and pilgrimage accounts, the extraordinary interaction between peasant economy and Russian mercantilist economy are varied aspects of studies about a widely scattered Kazakh domain. There are textual references about Volga-Tatar religious sphere, Tatar merchant colonies, Cossacks' encounters with the Kazakhs and community interaction between Kazakhs, Bashkirs and Astrakhan Karakalpaks. Despite an overall recognition of the spiritual assembly's authority (in terms of dispute resolution and other matters) in the pre-1917 period by the village *ulema* in the Volga-Tatar territory that was identified as the Kazakh Inner Horde domain, a very specific kind of community networking, i.e. a civil will prevailed within the *mahallah* (community). It aserted the status nd position of the religious functionaries like the *imam*, *mullah*, the *abid* (worshipper), the *akhund* (honorific title of someome learned in religious matters) who acted as the liaison officer and corresponded with the *imams* at the district level. A pattern of district-level Islamic education was introduced that comprised Quaranic reciters called the *Shagird* and junior instructors called Mu'adhdhin or *Muezin* (mosque official who summons the faithful to prayers from a minaret) and this was very different from the mainstream Muslim educational system.

Kazakh activism is also studied in relation to a process of revival of Kazakh spirituality in rural and urban areas. The idea is to review a situation in which despite a revival of Islamic religiosity, there has not been a complete radical turnaround and integration between communities prevailed. Scholars have been engaged in various methodological and empirical discussions about how Islam was not appropriated by a dominant Russian culture but how it continued to have linkages with the Russians throughout urban districts of Kazakhstan and how awareness about Islamic culture is expected to lead to an understanding of community identities that form a distinctive Kazakh national identity. This integrative formula, distinct from representations of 'anomie',[42] has inspired scholars to examine patterns of coexistence between Islam and Christianity. Spirituality in Kazakhstan implies a lifeway that was not competitive and hardly clashed with overall Russian interests of control and administration. Reflections on Catherine II's policy of religious toleration indicate an overall optimism in official circles about Islam. However, questions have also been raised about fundamental assumptions of Catherine's policies that treated Islam as a bulwark of the state. Without abandoning support for Islamic institutions elsewhere in the empire, tsarist authorities revised their policies of religious toleration in the steppe. On the one hand, there was an attempt to defend the *shariat* and on the other there was an attempt to align with the guardians of custom, i.e. *adat*. The realm of *adat* and the Russian attempt to administer religious sphere of activity through *biys* is the subject matter of Virginia Martin's study.[43] Some Russophone Kazakhs shared enthusiasm about Jadid 'enlightenment' in the steppe while others (Bukeikhanov et al.) were critical of Tatar influence and allied with Russian administration to administer the steppe and imbibe ideals of reform in the Kazakh way. Although there is scepticism about the religious policy that was pursued by the tsarist officials *vis-à-vis* the steppe's Muslim subjects, there was an atmosphere of relative ease and comfort as Muslim communities in the Russian empire also had the option of internal self-administration and their petitions were mostly granted.

The phenomenon of Islamization in the steppe and Central Asia has been a constant feature and scholarship tends to revolve round this aspect by not only quantifying the number of converts to the Islamic faith during the period 1860s to 1917 but also indicating features of a strong Islamic presence in south Kazakhstan. There is evidence of a huge presence of mosques, *madrasas* and *maktabs*, the growing influence of the *ulama*, the world of Islamic publishing, the blossoming of an Islamic discourse, a sufi Yasawi tradition that is preserved as collective religious memory in Turkistan. The reinterpretation of the image of Islam, the reference to the local Islamic traditions in Kazakhstan and the shared body of traditions and genres common to the Islamic world as a whole is the essence of new generation revivalist literature. The purpose is also to demonstrate the intellectual autonomy of the Muslim scholars of the steppe, whose debates took place within an Islamic context and milieu. In imperial Russia, none of these institutions were funded by the state, either at the imperial, provincial or local level. Rather, they were always privately funded, often at the village level. Frank's study of some of these institutions in the Inner Horde territory indicates that some of these villages had their own mosques, own schools and own *alims* (teachers).

So, studies about Kazakh spirituality have dealt with two aspects: (a) an extremely negative position about the curtailment of religious freedom and persecution of spiritual leaders during the tsarist era; (b) an impulse to describe the interactions between the imperial government and Muslim elite and intellectuals. Connected to the second aspect is Robert Geraci's study that examines the motivation of the missionaries and the pedagogues,[44] Charles Steinwedel's study of politics and governance after 1905 through the subjects' active participation in everyday life[45] and Naganawa Norihiro's description of the role of local Muslims in reorganizing their *mahallas*, their parishes and Friday congregations through interaction with the state after 1905.[46] The mediatory role of the spiritual assemblies in Ufa and Orenburg is sometimes considered as over-assessment by Stephane Dudoignon.[47]

CONCLUSION: THE UNSPECIFIED

The Kazakh story here thus focuses on Kazakh individuality that is not wholly distanced from the Russian 'affair'. Another important factor that is related to Kazakh individuality is the borderland contacts, especially with China because Chinese borderland issues redirect a lot of attention towards China's non-Han population that includes the Kazakhs, Uyghurs, Kyrgyz and the Mongols. The sharing of geographical and cultural space between China's 'new frontier', i.e. Xinjiang and Central Asia leads to new representations of borderlands and Xinjiang's history tends to be neatly woven into an overall Central Asian historiography. This is what the research on *Uygurovedenia* is engaged in and the Uyghurs have secured a new position as a field of enquiry in Kazakh historiography and are treated in various formats. On the one hand, there is a very traditional approach that takes into consideration the Silk Road model and the influence of diverse routes that pass through Xinjiang towards South, South-East and Central Asia. Secondly, the recognition of Xinjiang's Turkic identity has been extended to a sea of Turko-Mongol identities and linkages that stretch the idea of a Turkic monolith to Kazakh and Siberian (Altai) locales. In Kazakhstan, 'Uyghur studies' tends to be an institutionalized field and is specifically addressed by historians of the Kazakh Academy of Sciences.[48] Their urge to renegotiate a Uyghur past was a sharp contrast to a Western sociologist's experience on Kazakh borderlands.[49] The sociological perspective of hybridity that bred cleavages in Kazakh borderlands is not acceptable to Kazakh academics who continue to be inspired by the doctrine of social diversity as a reflection of their steppe tradition. These varied inputs have given fresh direction to the domain of Kazakh borderlands. Cultural hybridization seems to be the issue at stake though Kazakh scholars are committed to renegotiate with their Chinese surroundings. The Uyghur identity is a problematic that is addressed with a host of other local identities. The local Uyghur framework is addressed as a special issue not only in writings about alternative non-Han identities in China but also in the discourse about overlapping Turkic identities and the legacy of oasis identities which gives the Uyghurs access to their affiliated groups in Central Asia, especially the Kazakhs. [50]

NOTES

1. There was a slow replacement of Slavic and other elites by a Kazakh-dominated nomenklatura.
2. Tsypylma Darieva, 'Recruiting for the Nation: Post-Soviet Transnational Migrants in Germany and Kazakhstan', in Eric Kasten (ed.), *Rebuilding Identities: Pathways to Reform in Post-Soviet Siberia*, vol. 2, entitled *Properties as Culture: Culture as Property*, Siberian Studies, Max Planck Institute for Social Anthropology, Halle/Saale, 2005.
3. The topics that gained attention were Kazakhs' nostalgia of the Russian past, respect for values in Kazakhstan and Azerbaijan, preferential treatment of Uyghur minorities and interaction between oases groups and communities in China. Farideh Heyat, 'Re-Islamisation in Kyrgyzstan: Gender, New Poverty and the Moral Dimension', *Central Asian Survey*, 23 (3-4), December 2004; Nayareh Tohidi, 'Guardians of the Nation: Women, Islam and Soviet Legacy of Modernization in Azerbaijan', in Herbery L. Bodman and Nayareh Tohidi (eds.), *Women in Muslim Societies: Diversity Within Unity*, Boulder, CO: Lynne Reiner Publications, 1998; Barry Sautman, 'Preferential Policies for Ethnic Minorities in China: The Case of Xinjiang', in William Safran (ed.), *National and Ethnoregional Identities in China*, London: Frank Cass Publishers, 1998.
4. N.E. Masanov et al., *Istoriya Kazakhstana, narody i kultury*, Almaty: Daik Press, 2001.
5. Olivier Roy, *The New Central Asia: The Creation of Nations*, London: I.B. Tauris, 2000, p. 18.
6. Sebastien Peyrose, 'The "Imperial Minority": An Interpretative Framework of the Russians in Kazakhstan in the 1990s', *Nationalities Papers*, vol. 36, no. 1, March 2008.
7. *Lad* criticizes the Kazakhs' khanate history and bluntly repeats Soviet arguments about Russian presence and Russia's civilizing mission. Peyrose, op. cit., p. 109.
8. Introductory chapter by Anatoly Khazanov and core chapters written by Peter Golden, Andre Wink, Thomas T. Allsen and others in Anatoly M. Khazanov and Andre Wink (eds.), *Nomads in the Sedentary World*, Richmond, Surrey: Curzon Press, 2001.
9. Bhavna Dave, *Kazakhstan: Ethnicity, Language and Power*, London: RoutledgeCurzon, p. 33.
10. Hilda Eitzen, 'Refiguring Ethnicity Through Conflicting Genealogies', *Nationalities Papers*, 26 (3), 1998, pp. 435-8.
11. S.E. Tolybekov, *Kochevoe Obshchestvo kazakov v XVII-nachale XX veka: politico-ekonomicheskii analiz*, Alma Ata: Izdatel'stvo Nauka, Kazakhskoi SSR, 1971.

12 Agyn Khairullovich Kazymzhanov and Keith Owen Tribble, 'The Political Tradition of the Steppe', *Nationalities Papers*, 26 (3), 1998, pp. 455-6.

13. Vadim Trepavlov, 'Altytuly: ostatki Nogaiskoi ordy v kazakhskikh stepyakh', *Viestnikh Evrazii*, no. 2 (13), 2001, pp. 33-44.

14. Bakhytnur Otarbayeva, 'A Brief History of the Kazak People', *Nationalities Papers*, 26 (3), 1998, p. 425.

15. Sandzhar Asfendiarov, *Istoriia Kazakstana (s drevneishikh vremen)*, Alma Ata, 1935 [quoted in Steven Sabol, *Russian Colonization and the Genesis of Kazak National Consciousness*, Houndmills, Basingstoke: Palgrave, Macmillan, 2003, p. 15].

16. Allen Frank, 'Islamic Transformation on the Kazakh Steppe, 1742-1917: Toward an Islamic History of Kazakhstan under Russian Rule', in Hayashi Tadayuki (ed.), *The Construction and Destruction of National Histories of Slavic Eurasia*, Sapporo: Slavic Research Center, Hokkaido University, 2003. Naganawa Norihiro, 'Molding the Muslim Community through Tsarist Administration: *Mahalla* under the Jurisdiction of the Orenburg Mohammedan Spiritual Assembly after 1905', *Acta Slavica Iaponica*, vol. 23, p. 101.

17. Participation in the will and instruction of the *tengri* (sky) is the first attribute of political power. Agyn Khairullovch Kazymzhanov and Keith Owen Tribble, 'The Political Tradition of the Steppe', *Nationalities Papers*, 26 (3), 1998, pp. 455-62.

18. Steven Sabol, 'Kazak Resistance to Russian Colonization: Interpreting the Kenesary Kasymov Revolt, 1837-47', *Central Asian Survey*, June/September, 2003, p. 237.

19. Mukhtar Auezov, *Abai* (Abridged version), Moscow: Progress Publishers, 1975. Part One is a description of Abay's childhood and his daredevil acts while Part II depicts Abay as the poet whose travels gave him the experience of the new world.

20. Steven Sabol, 'Kazak Resistance to Russian Colonization: Interpreting the Kenesary Kasymov Revolt, 1837-1847', *Central Asian Survey*, June/September, 2003, p. 231.

21. Robert D. Crews, *For Prophet and Tsar: Islam and Empire in Russia and Central Asia*, Cambridge, Massachusetts: Harvard University Press, 2006, p. 195.

22 There was destruction of forests and grasslands, decrease in the average size of peasant holdings, negative effects on soil fertility, loss of chernozem soil, etc. Articles by J. Pallot and I. Stebelsky point to the negative effects of colonization that was followed by open confrontation with the natives, 'frontiersmen', merchants and craftsmen who were outnumbered by the Russian peasants during the sixteenth, seventeenth and eighteenth centuries. I. Stebelsky, 'Agriculture and Soil Erosion

in the European Forest-steppe'; I. Stebelsky, 'The Frontier in Central Asia', J. Pallot, 'The Development of Peasant Landholding: From Emancipation to the Revolution', in James H. Bater and R.A. French (eds.), *Studies in Russian Historical Geography,* vol. 1, London: Academic Press, 1983.

23. Martha Brill Olcott, *The Kazakhs,* Stanford: Hoover Institution Press, 1987.
24. Peter Rottier,'The Kazakhness of Sedentarization: Promoting Progress as Tradition in Response to the Land Problem', *Central Asian Survey,* 22 (1), March 2003, p. 70.
25. Willard Sunderland, 'Peasant Pioneering: Russian Peasant Settlers Describe Colonization and the Eastern Frontier, 1880s-1910', *Journal of Social History*, Summer 2001.
26. N.E. Nikitin. 'Voennosluzhiliye lyudi: I Sibiri v XVII veke', *Istoriya SSSR*, no. 2, 1980.
27. David Collins, 'Russia's Conquest of Siberia: Evolving Russian and Soviet Historical Interpretations', *European Studies Review*, 12(1), 1982.
28. Rottier, op. cit.
29. Uyama Tomohiko, 'A Strategic Alliance between Kazakh Intellectuals and Russian Administrators: Imagined Communities in Dala Walayatining Gazeti (1888-1902)', in Hayashi Tadayuki (ed.), *The Construction and Deconstruction of National Histories in Slavic Eurasia*, Sapporo: Slavic Research Center, Hokkaido University, 2003.
30. Uyama Tomohiko, 'The Geography of Civilizations: A Spatial Analysis of the Kazakh Intelligentsia's Activities, from the Mid-19th Century to the Early 20th Century', Kimitaka Matsuzato (ed.), *Regions: A Prism to View the Slavic Eurasian World: Towards a Discipline of Regionology,* Sapporo: Slavic Research Center, Hokkaido University, 2000, chapter 3, p. 70.
31. Tomohiko, 'The Geography of Civilizations....'. op. cit. In his concluding remarks, Tomohiko points out that the Kazakh intellectuals expressed diverse opinions and behavioural patterns though they were in favour of a common ideology at least till 1913 and as a core group were able to organize a nation-wide movement.
32. Isabelle Kreindler, 'Ibrahim Altynsaryn, Nikolai Ilminskii and the Kazakh National Awakening', *Central Asian Survey,* 2(3), 1983, p. 100.
33. He was the great grandson of Ablai Khan of the eighteenth century whose exercise of political authority is legendary.
34. Kermit E. McKenzie, 'Chokan Valikhanov: Kazakh Princeling and Scholar', *Central Asian Survey,* 8(3), 1989, pp. 7-8.
35. Uyama Tomohiko, '"Devotion to the People" and Paternalistic Authoritarianism Among Qazaq Intellectuals, from the Mid-nineteenth

Century to 1917', in Stephane A. Dudoignon (ed.), *Devout Societies vs. Impious States?: Transmitting Islamic Learning in Russia, Central Asia and China Through the Twentieth Century* (Proceedings of an international colloquium held in the Carre des Sciences, French Ministry of Research, Paris, 12-13 November 2001), Berlin: Klaus Schwarz Verlag, 2004, p. 21.

36. Adeeb Khalid's study of aspects of Muslim cultural reform deals with this subject of varieties of reform. Stephane Dudoignon also explores the patterns of *maktab* reform that preceded *jadid* reformism of the Tatars. Adeeb Khalid, *The Politics of Muslim Cultural Reform: Jadidism in Central Asia*, Berkeley: University of California Pess, 1998; Stephane A. Dudoignon, 'Djadidisme, mirasisme, islamisme', in *Cahiers du Monde Russe*, vol. XXXVII (1-2), 1996.
37. There is hardly much information about Kazakh political activity in the steppe prior to the 1905 revolution. Martha Brill Olcott, *The Kazakhs,* Stanford, California: Hoover Institution Press, 1987, p. 110.
38. Dina Amanzhalova, 'Kazakhskaia avtonomiia: ot zamysla natsionalov k samoopredeleniyu po-Sovietski', *Acta Slavica Iaponica*, vol. 21, 2004.
39. Norihiro, op. cit.
40. Ibid., p. 101.
41. Allen J. Frank, *Muslim Religious Institutions in Imperial Russia: The Islamic World of Novouzensk District and the Kazakh Inner Horde, 1780-1910*, Leiden: Brill, 2001. Introductory chapter introduces the subject on local Islamic institutions and local texts that are valuable source material on the local histories of the steppe before 1917.
42. The concept *anomie* was used by early sociologists like Emile Durkheim (1893) to describe changes in society produced by the Industrial Revolution. The term is now used to describe a state of society, referring to characteristics of the social system, not of individuals, although individuals were affected by this force. In the twentieth century, *anomie* is used to represent a state of disaffection or disconnectedness and has assumed a more social psychological meaning. Edgar F. Borgatta and Rhonda J.V. Montgomery (eds.), *Encyclopedia of Sociology*, vol. 1, Macmillan Reference USA, 2000, pp. 164-7.
43. Virginia Martin, *Law and Custom in the Steppe: The Kazakhs of the Middle Horde and Russian Colonialism in the Nineteenth Century*, Richmond, Surrey: Curzon, 2001.
44. Robert Geraci, *Window on the East: National and Imperial Identities in Late Tsarist Russia*, Ithaca and London: Cornell University Press, 2001.
45. Charles Steinwedel, 'The 1905 Revolution in Ufa: Mass Politics, Elections, and Nationality', *Russian Review*, vol. 59, no. 4, October 2000.

46. Norihiro's article deals with the positive milieu in the aftermath of 17 April 1905 when toleration of faiths was proclaimed and the Manifesto of 17 October 1905 that was perceived as a restoration of the tradition of Empress Catherine II. After the 1905 reforms, the Muslims were encouraged to put forth their demands in the state Dumas and the three special conferences during 1906-14 developed as petition campaigns of the Muslims. Norihiro, op. cit.
47. Stephane A. Dudoignon, 'Un Islam peripherique? Quelques reflexions sur la presse musulmane de Siberi a la veille de la PremiereGuerre Mondiale', *Cahiers du Monde Russe.*
48. *Aktual'nye prbemy sovremennovo Uygurovedeniya (Materialy mezhdunarodnoi konferentsii posvyaschennoy 50-letniyu Uygurovedeniya v Kazakhstane),* Almaty, 2002.
49. Sean Roberts, the Western sociologist who travelled on a bus along the Kazakh border from Khorgus to Kuldja gives an account of the Uyghur dispassionateness towards everybody and a hybrid Chinese-Kazakh conscience that is reflective of the ambiguity of the *khitailiklar-sovietliklar* dichotomy. Sean Roberts, 'The Uighurs of the Kazakh Borderlands: Migration and the Nation', *Nationalities Papers*, vol. 26, no. 3, 1998, pp. 519-20.
50. Dru Gladney, 'Relational Alterity: Constructing Dungan (Hui), Uygur, and Kazakh Identities across China, Central Asia and Turkey', *History and Anthropology*, 9 (4), 1996 and Justin J. Rudelson, *Oasis Identities: Uyghur Nationalism Along China's Silk Road*, New York: Columbia University Press, 1997 cited in M. Cristina Cesaro, 'Walking a tightrope: A Quest for Uyghur Identity', in Giampiero Bellingeri and Giovanni Pedrini (eds.), *Central Asia: A Decade of Reforms, Centuries of Memories*, Venice: Dipartimento do Studi Eurasiatici, Universita Ca' Foscari di Venezia, 2004, p. 197.

CHAPTER 3

The Siberian Domain

INTRODUCTION: WHY SIBERIA?

Topics like the Eurasian frontier as an interactive space and the domain of Kazakh nomads as Golden Horde and Middle Horde descendants lead us to ponder about similar such self-sufficient dynamic locales within the vast belt of steppe territory stretching from the borders of Hungary to Manchuria and which became the epicenter of what was called a 'drama of Eurasian history'.[1] The drama was shaped in an era when the pastoral people inhabiting this area since the second millennium BC were engulfed by agricultural people with whom the nomad herders and hunters were engaged in a natural competition for economic resources. The human drama in this steppe zone (which dates back to the twelfth century) and its resultant effect—the defeat of the nomad conquerors by sedentary invaders—was a feature of the dominant narrative that focused on the sedentary cultures and seldom dealt with other aspects of the vibrant environment. The re-emergence of historical geography as a prominent field of research that examines the human environment as an interactive space and not as a combative sphere of influence has generated interest in the steppe's extended boundaries in the west, east and south. The attention automatically shifts to south Siberia and its Inner Asian environs which also share the steppe features of dry grasslands that are insulated by mountain chains of the

Tienshan and the Altai. The present study therefore is concerned with Siberia not as an exclusively Russian domain (because a great majority of Siberia's inhabitants are Russians or because the Russians made Siberia their special administrative unit) but as an Asian borderland that had pre-Tsarist transcontinental links with Mongolia, China and Central Asia. This aspect, i.e. the aspect of Siberia as a vibrant steppe ecosystem will be examined in this essay.

In the recent past, however, interest has been aroused in the role of the indigenous people of Siberia which does give an impression of opinions outside the Russian framework. A review of Siberia's recorded history sometimes adds another significant angle to steppe historiography—that the Siberians belonged to the Tatar domain, a proto-Turkic stronghold and a Mongol commonwealth that survived till the thirteenth century. The disintegration of the Golden Horde into the khanates of Crimea, Astrakhan, Kazan, Nogai and Siberia, the foundations of the Siberian khanate on the banks of the river Irtysh also received some coverage in secondary literature of the 1990s and what we have before us is a template or a mosaic of Turko-Mongol identities that cannot be confined to the formula of trade and raid. The barbarian paradigm is contested in a series of works that have tried to study the nomadic terrain as a patchwork of local authorities that proliferated at the rim of sedentary empires. Scholars are interested in post-Chingizid alliances and the political dispensation under Turko-Tatar semi-suzerains of the Siberian khanate on the banks of the Tobolsk and the Irtysh.[2] These revelations about Siberia's Asiatic component are sub-sets and categories that are distinct from the dominant narrative about European Russia's military conquest in south Russia and the complex managerial system of the Tsarist era after Kulomzin launched his Slavic peasant settlement policy and Witte launched his decade-long railroad project, the Trans-Siberian Railroad.

The collapse of this frontier dispensation in the wake of the Yermak expedition of 1581 opens up the saga of 'discovery of

Siberia' by Russia.[3] Gradually the image of the region as a continental landmass that constituted the core of a rapidly expanding imperial system acquired prominence. The subject of imperial control is being reviewed in the context of the nineteenth-century European intellectual mindset and several geographical images of the non-European world are in vogue. There is an attempt to deconstruct the 'perceptible reality' of the regions in question, bringing to light a series of intellectual debates about how a region should be represented. The Russian intellectuals' visions about Siberia as the geographical other and the discrete images or image clusters about Siberia that emerged in the cultural thought process of European Russia in the nineteenth century are being examined. This questioning has taken place largely in the fields of historical geography and social anthropology. The geographical understanding of *novaya zemlya* tends to be more meaningful than in the past and at the very centre of this debate is Mark Bassin's idea of representing spaces. Bassin dwells on nineteenth-century imperial visions about space in juxtaposition to nationalist visions about the Russian East. Bassin compares Siberia's reality with the exiles' romantic image of Siberia as wilderness. The reality-myth dilemma comes to sharper focus in a re-evaluation of imperial Russian literature that refers to Siberia as *prostor* which has two meanings: (a) vastness, unlimited space and (b) liberty and freedom, which was depicted by exiles about vast lands beyond the Urals.[4] The latter view comes closest to Frederick Jackson Turner's position about an advancing frontier from which Siberian historians are deriving a lot of inspiration today. Their writings indicate a deep sense of belonging to the region not merely as a Russian subset but also as an independent category. Another dimension is the sociological perspective. Sociologists have examined Siberia's human angle, the lifeways and traditions among Siberian communities which they protect as their 'cultural property'.[5] The sociological and historical perspectives are sometimes neatly woven together.

The literature that has appeared so far is not just a mixture of Soviet romanticism and idealization of a boom zone and post-Soviet critique of gargantuan projects that were abandoned during the Stalinist period. Such perspectives about Siberia indicate a flexible stance rather than a rigid overview of a vast, unwieldy space. Siberia is no longer considered to be an elusive country beyond the Urals where exiles and criminals operate through their networks. This also leads to the polemical debate about the 'paradise' that Siberia represents. Siberia's vibrant ecosystem has become the showpiece of Eurasia's environmental diversity and habitat. Siberia's energy sector concentrated in Russia's far east tends to be the focal point of regional studies that deal with parameters of eastward integration and issues of Russian federalism. The casual glimpse at Siberia as the exotic landmass extending from the Urals in the west to the Pacific Ocean in the east that have been traversed by raiders on horses and pilgrims on foot is a very lopsided view of a dynamic region that has a lot of romantic appeal. The grand expeditions of men-on-spot who have been on the perennial quest of riverine trade routes beyond the Urals and fixed their gaze on the European markets via the maritime belt in the Yenisei region are strikingly relevant today. These expeditions symbolize Siberia's connectivity from Moscow to Vladivostok via Beijing, Krasnoyarsk and Ulan Ude or Tomsk. For such explorers, Siberia was a revelation and represented the future. For casual travellers, Siberia is a once-in-a-while experience.[6] Today's culture-enthusiasts are trying to retrace the railway route of the Trans-Siberian Railway and reflect on Siberia as a heritage site and cultural spectacle of the lifeways and traditions of the Arctic, sub-Arctic Tundra, Taiga, steppe and the maritime belt.[7] In all respects Siberia is a reference point and an ideal setting that once stirred the dreams of warriors, settlers, merchants, intellectuals, pilgrims and migrants.

What is exclusively treated is the economic dimension, especially the economic prospects of a Siberian neighbourhood. The Far East and the Far North were classic examples of this approach and the idea was to question several 'givens' about Tsarist Russia's fur trade interests (which were never consistent), tribute exaction in the Far North, Russia's individualistic maritime interests in the Far East juxtaposed to an integration formula that became very popular towards the end of the Soviet period. The sensitivity about integration is revealed in assertions about a market-driven strategy in the Pacific littoral.[8] The significance of the Pacific as the 'meeting point' of Russian and American interests and the convergence of satellite states was highlighted.[9] The system of industrial governance in Siberian towns that grew up in and around the Trans-Siberian Railroad and the growth of an industrial proletariat became the source of pride for citizens based in Omsk, Novosibirsk and Irkutsk and a cause for inter-town rivalries and regional antagonism.[10] Industrialization of the Tomsk *guberniya* during the Soviet era was an offshoot of the Tsarist initiatives. Case studies about industrial geography in the Tsarist period highlight industrial activities (mining and smelting) in the Tomsk guberniya in the pre-1917 period.[11] Growing awareness about Tsarist and Soviet industrial performances and the phenomenon of connectivity through transportation corridors, a subject which has been addressed by Siberian economists, have added extra importance to western and eastern Siberia as prime export-import hubs, raising prospects of alliance-building with her Asiatic neighbours (Japan, Mongolia, China and Kazakhstan) as well as with Europe.[12] Japanese scholars are not unaware about the possibilities about Siberia's emergence as a meso-area and the congregation of triadic identities.[13] Despite this euphoria, questions are raised within the domain of economic geography prompting experts to ponder about Siberia as a non-accessible zone in terms of the distance from Moscow. It has stimulated the debate about the potency of regionology/regionalism and has challenged the hypothesis about Siberia as a federal alternative.

Soviet and post-Soviet representations of Siberia's regional history reflect solid ground analysis. In Soviet times, here was an irresistible urge to deal with what the literature of the region represented. Anatole G. Mazour, the specialist historian on Russian and Soviet historiographical traditions, reviewed the character of historical writing and provided a detailed account of the professional atmosphere during the Soviet period. Mazour writes about the classical Soviet model of focusing on 'periodizations' of history.[14] There was a shift of methodology at every stage of 'historical enquiry' in the Soviet Union. The disciplining of history by the Communist Party was a recurrent issue and historians were 'instructed' to provide factual representations of history on almost every aspect that the Communist ideologues could think about. The study of sources (*istochnikovdenie*) had a wide appeal and state academies played a vital role in popularizing the tradition of learning and re-learning historical sources on matters related to feudal development, commercial growth, demographic patterns, and so on. The role of the Soviet publishing world in disseminating ideas about socialist reconstruction in Siberia and the conveyance of historiographical tradition through Party-supported journals (*Voprosy Istorii* and *Istoriya SSSR*) have been amply indicated. The perspective was about a region in the making—peasant role and agricultural development were special features of agrarian history while the growth of towns and city-based statistical surveys were milestones in urban development that were evenly represented since the 1960s. The present chapter will seek to address some of these variant moods and perspectives on Siberia which on the whole have expanded the domain of Siberian studies. The idea is to present the long and the short—Siberia represents a collage of ideas that tends to resurrect the region from its monochromatic Russian framework. In scholarly debates about Eurasianism, Siberia has assumed significance as a geopolitical and geo-cultural space, representing both Russia and Asia. This essay has a two-way approach: (a) to focus on Siberia as integral to the dominant narrative, and (b) to pinpoint the departures from that dominant model.

INTRICACIES OF THE APPROACHES

The dominant narrative deals with Russian penetration into Siberia and transformation of a Turco-Tatar domain into a Slavic colony. The narrative focuses on a law-governed Russian system with inertia of growth and development because of the involvement of people in a range of activities—from trade to political sloganeering. The ideological orientation of the people was equally fascinating: the popular mood was reflected in the aspirations of the people about autonomy and development. A streamlined approach towards state-society relations indicate the state as the patron of magnanimous projects and the contours of growth were profiled along the lines of what and how the state administered. The society on the other hand was considered to be the agent of progress. It is within this framework of state patronage and social commitment that Siberia's relations with Russia has been analysed. Within that frame of Russian history, there is an attempt to depict Siberia as Tsarist Russia's trade zone (or fur zone) which in the sixteenth century was a tract of 'alien' territory encompassing 4,000 miles of grasslands, mountains, forests and lakes east and south of the Urals. The focus gradually shifted to Siberia's migrant population, the service personnel (military men, expeditionists, geographers, artisans, gubernatorial-merchant elite)[15] that changed the social profile of a region earlier inhabited by Golden Horde descendants. There have been candid confessions of Siberia as Russia strengthened by observations about Siberia as a military colony, a zone of Russia's fur-trade ambitions and looking for market expansion in the Pacific. This zeal of discovering Siberia is associated with Russia's scientific-geographical missions in the east and the north in order to explore possible waterways of trade up to the mouth of the Ob.

The 'trade fever' was perennially present and the merchant chronicles give evidence of attractive furs east of the Pechora River, in what was called *Yugorskaia zemlitsa* or the land of the Yugors (present-day Khantis) and the Samoyeds.[16] Between the eleventh and fifteenth centuries, the Novgorod merchants established themselves in the fur-belt and extracted tributes from the local people of Komi territory or Yugrians. So, according to early annals of Siberian history, it was the Komi region close to the Urals that succumbed to Russian mercantilist gaze and the Novgorod merchants tried to reach the region through two prime river routes that passed through the Arctic region. The Novgoroders while penetrating the region clashed with the local communities and there was not much that could be said about them or the 'occupation' by Muscovite princes until a third party—the Tatar khanate of Sibir—emerged. It was the establishment of the khanate of Sibir on the banks of Irtysh, Tobolsk and Ob and the Turco-Tatar Khans' binding authority on the Komi territory that restricted fur trade operations of the Russians who as late entrants, by default became competitors of a lucrative fur trade that was already very much in demand in Central Asia and the Middle East as well as in China. It was the conquest of the Kazan khanate in 1552 that brought the Russians on a collision course with the Tatar Khans of Siberia far south. The latter were successors of resilient groups among the Yenisei Kyrgyz and the Kipchak Turks and received support from breakaway Turkic factions of the Nogai Horde. The challenge of the Russians from the north was not to be tolerated by the Tatar Khans of Sibir, especially as the Russian tsars started concentrating on utilizing the khanate of Sibir as a thoroughfare on the legendary caravan route that linked Kazan with Central Asia by way of Perm, Irtysh and the Kipchak steppe. The extinction of Perm opened the floodgates of Russian intervention and the Stroganov merchant family entrenched itself on Perm soil with state support. James Forsyth gives an account of the Stroganov phenomenon and the family's strong links with the Muscovite state:

> Like other pioneers in frontier lands where the state wanted to establish a Russian population, the Stroganovs were granted immunity from taxes and customs dues for twenty years. On the other hand, they accepted responsibility for the defence of Russian settlements and the frontier of

Muscovy against attack by Nogai and other hordes. For this purpose they were permitted to erect fortified towns and maintain soldiers with fire-arms. The rights and privileges which Stroganov was granted made him practically the governor of the Kama region, and soon provided him the opportunity to extend his private enterprise, and the frontier of the Tsar's realm, beyond the Urals into Siberia.[17]

The Stroganov merchants were protected by Cossack desperadoes who belonged to staunch Orthodox faith and stalked the Ukrainian steppe and challenged the authority of the Crimean Tatars and Turks in the sixteenth century. Cossack daredevilry is a legend and has inspired fiction writers like Harold Lamb to fictionalize their guts, grit and heroism.[18] It was because of Cossack presence that Siberia in the sixtgeenth century became one huge military camp with a sprinkling of *voevodas* and *ostrogi* (fortresses).[19] Siberia was also a giant business enterprise because of Stroganovs' links with the Chancellery. This narrative emphasizes merchant contacts and Cossack military back-up of the Russian regime.

Russian penetration of Siberia received maximum attention in sources recounting events in the military occupation of south Russia. The turning point of Siberia's history, as suggested by Soviet annals, was conquest and raid—and participants' sources that corroborated evidence on these aspects received full attention. The idea was to disseminate information about institutions and institution-builders. *Istoriya Sibiri* (the five-volume work on Siberia's history) is a classic example of Soviet historiography's emphasis on source-based analysis. The Stroganov chronicle, the Yesipov chronicle and the Remezov chronicle were cited as principal sources on the Yermak campaign.[20] Each of the chronicles has its own emphasis—the Stroganov document is an assertion of military might; the Yesipov chronicle reflects on the religious aspect of Yermak's campaign and in particular emphasizes the role of the Orthodox Church, the unnamed Remezov chronicle, rich in illustrations, indicates the preparations for the campaign by Yermak (mostly boats and stores) and also bears evidence about Maksim Stroganov's direct links with the campaigners. The chronicles furnish details about the route of Yermak starting from Verkhotur'ye, a major shipyard for Siberian traffic. The route was not a pioneering one because it was in regular use by the Russians who had already made considerable headway in inland navigation. There is substantial information on the mode of travel (flat-bottomed vessels called *doschaniks* capable of carrying men and provisions). There seems to be adequate evidence about the Stroganov family being intimately connected with Yermak's expedition and is said to have sponsored Yermak, his son Timofey and his Volga *atamans*, his comrade Ivan Koltso in building boats that would be used against the enemy force of Kuchum Khan who fought on land. Maksim and Nikita Stroganov are said to have promoted the fighters by providing them ample food and drink in their strongholds as they approached the Siberian land on the Irtysh River. The Cossack bands resorted to ambush from the rivers, occasionally alighting at cross-channels (loops of rivers) to camp during the night. Such a strategy was foiled by Kuchum Khan who spied on them and ambushed them at the river joint. Yermak managed to escape Kuchum's sword, fled on a boat towards the river but could not reach it because the distance was too great. Wounded, he fell into on the river and drowned. Yermak's death was followed by the departure of the other Cossack leaders who reassembled again in the Tura and Irtysh rivers and gradually established strongholds on the Ob River where they settled during winter. There were occasional skirmishes with Siberian princes on the Tobolsk but finally it was with the help of the Muscovite princes that the Siberian prince Seydek was overpowered. Exaction in the form of fur tribute was resumed all over the Siberian khanate and the proceeds went to the Novgorod treasury. The narrative of the campaign indicates that it was engineered by the Stroganovs with Cossack military back-up. It also indicates the stiff resistance by Kuchum's successors to reoccupy their lands on the Irtysh River. The Moscow princes made a belated entry and spread Christianity on Siberian soil and commanded the exaction of fur tribute which dealt the final blow to the khanate.[21] A brigand like Yermak became a legend as a military commander and memories of Kuchum Khan as the lone Siberian khan, resolutely fighting the Russians for 16 years to restore his Siberian khanate (a process that began with his refusal to pay tribute to the conquering forces) slowly faded. Yermak succeeded and Kuchum failed—this is the basic theme of the narratives on the campaign. Yermak's campaign is remembered more as a private Cossack affair because it was not engineered from Moscow. At the same time, the campaign seems to be a continuation of Russia's policy of control—Moscow was using her 'pioneers' to tame adversaries and to control the routes of Russian advance into the region bordering the steppe.[22] In a recent publication, the Cossack component of Russian imperial history has been re-examined and poignant memories of a warrior class and a service community with diasporic contacts have breathed new life in a sea of war-memoirs. As warriors on horseback they became an asset for the Muscovite princes and a great source of strength for the White forces of Ataman Dutov during the Russian Civil War. The Cossack community was associated not only with military activism but also with missionary activities and entrepreneurship that stretched the entire territory on both sides of the Urals. Retrospective analysis suggests that the Cossacks were not maniacal warriors and subjugators of the Siberian Khans or adjuncts of the imperial Russian force, but a community of believers, intellectuals and businessmen with worldwide contacts.[23]

The story of Russia's expansion in Asia climaxed with accounts of Russia's expeditions in the Pacific littoral. The prime strategic concern of the Russian state was to settle on what was recognized as 'empty' and 'bleak' territory east of the Urals, particularly in the Amur-Ussuri sector of Transbaikalia that was inhabited by non-Russians such as Cossacks, Chinese and Koreans. Mountainous Transbaikalia was devoid of land and water transport and remained a barrier that separated the Russian far east from the resource-abundant central Siberia. Besides, Russia's Pacific Rim was considered vulnerable in the face of Chinese and Japanese competition as well as Britain's diplomatic manoeuvring on maritime territory. In light of these developments, the defence of Russian territory on the maritime territory in the east was considered most important. In fact, the Sino-Siberian border and the Amur region became the main zone of geographical intelligence gathering and mapping. Cartographic developments in the seventeenth and eighteenth centuries indicated that map-making was a major preoccupation of the Russian military department. The nineteenth-century Russian maps traced the riverine arteries of trade in the China sector and made enquiries about the Amur River network, depicting Tartary as a major entrepôt of trade. Cartography was a major tool for military geographers of the nineteenth century and the desire to obtain foolproof information about the Pacific frontier that merged with the borderlands of East Siberia, Mongolia and the Far East was the major concern of the Russian military circles. Mark Bassin's study of the Great Siberian Expedition (1855-63) reflects the mid-nineteenth-century mindset among Russian geographers to study the Russian fatherland in general and more specifically Russian Asia.[24] The vision of Russian messianism in Asia heightened and the nationalist urge was to open up 'a vast new panorama for Russian activity'. It was with this messianic conviction that Russia began its expansion in the second half of the nineteenth century into the Far East and Central Asia and conducted geographical explorations there.

Another aspect of the dominant narrative is Siberia's Railroad experience. The imagination of Siberia as a spatial identity began with the establishment of the Trans-Siberian Railroad, which historian Steven Marks calls European Russia's 'Road to Power'.[25] Marks' biography of the Trans-Siberian Railroad points to a long-planned Tsarist diplomatic exercise in order to connect the eastern and western ends of the empire.[26] The rationale for building the railroad in the 1890s under the aegis of the Russian Finance Minister Sergei Witte (though its actual creation was preceded by extensive planning about railroads and bureaucratic debate in the 1860s through to the 1880s) was economic development. But it was the presence of China and more particularly Chinese railroad constructions in Manchuria that led Russian military circles to take the decision of building a railroad with principal connectors.

The Turner influence on Siberia's railroad doctrine is also being examined which unfolds the comparative framework of North American and Russian frontiers. The frontier as a decisive space had already made its mark in intellectual circles of America and Russia in the mid-nineteenth century. The post-industrialization phase had opened up prospects of integration of distant frontiers and the construction of great transcontinental railroads through the North American continent and the Eurasian hinterland proved to be an important instrument to integrate vast dominions into a unitary empire. Like the Union Pacific railroad, the Trans-Siberian counterpart was an ambitious project with enormous national prestige. *Vostochnoe Obozrenie*, the journal of Siberian regionalists, enthusiastically supported the Siberian experiment. The railroad became a huge enterprise for Russian engineers who travelled to the US and Canada in order to be acquainted with technological know-how.

How the Trans-Siberian Railroad impacted on the imagination of the people is also an interesting subject of analysis. It was not only a magnificent venture but a realistic experience too. The railroad did not only symbolize the power game of the Russian authorities, but also became the showpiece of a visually reconstructed Russia. The panorama of a huge Eurasian landmass experienced by travellers on 'a virtual voyage' of the Trans-Siberian Railroad became a subject of analysis. Artists painted the moveable panorama on canvas that attracted a lot of attention in international exhibitions. The train became a symbolic showpiece of the economic power of Russia. It not only represented a landscape that was exploited through agriculture and mining but also transgressed cultural borders from Europe to Asia, borders that became united through technical skill and prowess and imperial dominance.[27]

In Russian literary representations, the Transsib has been portrayed as an artery that joins the furthest extremes of European Russia and its far eastern territory. It was a project that not only symbolized technological advancement and land connectivity but also impacted on the intellectuals' imagining of a neglected landscape. The visual transformation of Russia through the Transsib has appealed to the Russian literary world in many ways. According to poet Khlebnikov, the Trans-Siberian Railroad became the metaphor of life. In the poet's imagination, there was a 'tree-train' on the railroad that was not a mere machine that rumbled and roared, but symbolized a living organism—it was a tree of life for the people of Russia as it changed their way of life. Asia re-emerged from the spatial trope of imperial neglect or imperial domination because of the Transsib that gave both European and Asiatic parts of Russia their new identities. Feodor Dostoevsky identified railroads going into Asia as crucial steps towards 'breaking away' from the Eurocentric mould. Both Dostoevsky and Khlebnikov revised the portrait of Siberia—the Transsib was a reality that touched people's lives. As the Transsib rolled on, the literature on Siberia became more and more focused on the Eurasian space that was being recast, reconfigured and modernized.[28] So, the overall perceptions of Asia changed because of the railroad culture. Ideas about a chaotic steppe frontier inhabited by nomads of the Mongol tribe (Buryats, Kazakhs and Kalmyks) were replaced by an overall appreciation of the real world of the East which was an exposition of nomads' lives. The Transsib thus is the central theme of an alternative discourse that tries to break away from the paradigmatic notion of Siberia as an uninhabited space with binary oppositions between the forest and the steppe, nomad and the settler. The endurance of the traveller on the Transsib is reflected in the literature that eulogizes the railroad. According to the popular nineteenth-century Russian writer Anton Chekhov, the journey to the Russian Far East was a 'culturological enigma'. His acquaintance with Asiatic Russia and his memories about Sakhalin as the furthest eastern frontier of Mother Russia unfolds the Russian literary world's nostalgic impressions of a far-flung empire. Chekhov's personal experiences were recounted in post-Soviet writings about land connectivity.[29] His impressions of travel were totally different from the viewpoint of weary commercial travellers like Eric Newby. Newby visited the region in 1977 and was awfully critical of the Transsib as the longest railway in the world, with very little stopovers for foreigners (only in Novosibirsk, Irkutsk and Khabarovsk) that made the journey more arduous than imagined. His impressions of the railroad were negative, the only positive feature being the enchanting view of the Baraba Steppe—an Asiatic frontier beyond Novosibirsk—which with its Kazakh-Kyrgyz-Mongol-Kalmyk population remained disconnected from the prosperous Slavic industrial and commercial centres like Irkutsk.[30]

Another aspect of the dominant discourse is the subject of peasant colonization and settlement (*pereselenie*) of the nineteenth century after the abolition of serfdom in 1861—a subject that is intrinsically related to Russification and which, according to the first census report of 1897, had a migration volume that is unmatched. According to current assessments, the drive also reflects a settler psyche and not the imperial mission as such.

There was a burgeoning literature on the peasant colonization of Siberia.[31] The man in charge of this mission was Anatoly N. Kulomzin (1838-1924), a rather unconventional bureaucrat who had a Victorian mind and was totally committed to the enhancement of governmental status. Kulomzin was entrusted by Sergei Witte, the finance minister with the responsibility of managing the committee of the Siberian Railroad. He was also placed in charge of auxiliary enterprises associated with the Trans-Siberian and coordination of peasant settlement was one principal task. Witte and Kulomzin were intent on solidifying governmental control and expediting the process of unification of a country that was under the grip of separatism in the peripheries. The idea of a 'monolithic nationalist empire' and the *Rechtstaat*

European model resulted in a fundamental shift in official policy which was oriented towards railroad construction and peasant resettlement programmes. Kulomzin was an expert in Russian peasant matters and was keen to involve the peasants of Russia in *zemstvo* activities, but in a land that was far removed from the forest heartland of Muscovy. The purpose was to stop centrifugal tendencies especially because regional sentiments were striking deep roots in the rubric of Russia and the suspicion about Siberian separatists was looming large. Also, the rhetoric of a Yellow Peril in ruling circles and growing engagements of Chinese and Korean traders in the local trade of the Far East and the growing demographic disparity in that region caused concern and Kulomzin, a sober-minded official became wary of what he felt was 'a glaring deficiency of Russian dominion in Siberia'. Siberia in his opinion represented a classic example of 'overgovernment at the centre and underadministration in the provinces'.

Kulomzin's 1896 and 1897 trips beyond the Urals led to his aspiration for building grain centres of the North American type in the Siberian Black Earth zone. To augment Russian presence in the far-flung territories of Russia, Kulomzin ventured on his peasant resettlement programme. There is an interesting observation that Kulomzin was actually moving away from Russian policy of military administration and was trying to upgrade provincial life of Russia by giving it a planned look. The immediate cause of the resettlement drive was the agricultural crisis of European Russia in the mid-nineteenth century—the post-1861 abolition of serfdom which resulted in oppression by the landlords and 'land-hunger' of peasants. Large numbers of peasants, 'emancipated' after 1861, were driven by poverty to set out on the long journey to Siberia on the Moscow *trakt* which was a continuous route, a highroad from the Urals to Irkutsk and beyond that became operational in 1763. The massive expansion in Russian peasant settlement[32] resulted in what David Moon calls the expansion of Russia's political frontier and the conjoining of other important facets—the life-way frontier, the environmental frontier and hierarchical frontier.[33] The completion of the Trans-Siberian Railroad around Lake Baikal opened up the Far East for further settlement. The most popular region for migration was the black-earth region of the Tomsk province between the Irtysh, Ob and Altai mountains and the greatest number of migrants were Russians, Ukrainians and Belorussians (about 85 per cent). The rest included 'unassimilated indigenous communities' (about 11 per cent), convicts and exiles, prisoners-of-war and the 'the undesirable people' (about 4 per cent) who thronged the gold-mining belts of the Altai and Tomsk regions, the Angara and Yenisei valleys. Even Jews and Tatars who had reached Siberia in the 1830s (the former as convicts and the latter, mainly Kazan Tatars seeking refuge because of rising poverty at home) were a characteristic of Russian town life in the late nineteenth century. According to statistics of the late nineteenth century, the Jews became a sizeable community, and there were Jewish enclaves in Ekaterinburg, Chelyabinsk, Tobolsk, Omsk, Tomsk, Irkutsk and Chita. They functioned as craftsmen and like the Poles, contributed to the economic development of the colony. The same was true of the Kazan Tatars who concentrated in the Baraba steppe region, engaging as merchants specializing in grain, salt or leather trade. Empirical evidence about community distribution can thus lead to varying interpretations about Russians as a settler colony in Siberia. It is an exaggeration to suggest that Siberia was exclusively Russian. There were in fact a number of strains within the Russian society[34] that is often not taken into account while referring to peasant infiltration as a linear process.

The peasant voice is another subject of analysis. The imperial mission and a peasant drive to settle on unknown territory were not necessarily correlated. Siberia's historians have also challenged the hypothesis about difficult conditions arguing that there were cases of resettlement and internal migration which furthered the process of colonization and early settlers moved from original places of settlement to the Far East. In other words, contrary to what was regarded as growing dissatisfaction among settlers about 'unknown territory', one tends to get a better view of the prospects that actually emerged leading to relocation, resettlement and internal migration. Leonid Goryushkin, a prominent Siberian historian and his Western counterpart William Sunderland have concentrated on these internal settings and their studies have expanded the scope of study of Russian peasant settlement. Sunderland's study of settler literature indicates that the peasant settlers were guided by practical concerns and local horizons. The great majority of peasants who resettled to the borderlands in the late imperial period came from predominantly agricultural provinces in the central black earth region and left-bank Ukraine and were already accustomed to seasonal migrations (*otkhod*) but could never make their ends meet on the farm. So, it was lack of sufficient land and poor harvests that prompted peasants from the western side of the Urals to proceed towards the direction of Siberia. Also, the Trans-Siberian Railroad was expected to make relocation quicker and cheaper and migrants (mostly classified as poor peasants) moved over to lands that were not in the real sense, too far away (in western Siberia and the Kazakh steppe and further on to Russian Central Asia) and were the easiest and least expensive to reach. The principal places of settlement in the early 1890s were the Tomsk *guberniya*, the Akmolinsk (now Tselinograd) *oblast* and the Yeneseinsk *guberniya*. They selected their places in accordance with the recommendation of the scouts who were sent to reconnoitre suitable plots of land or of earlier migrants. So what is presupposed as unplanned and unrestricted migration needs to be reconsidered primarily because of this scouting arrangement which allowed the peasant settlers to be sufficiently informed about their destination. They naturally preferred to congregate in areas near the lakes and rivers, or near forest belts which had similar conditions of settlement as in European Russia.[35] It was easier for the settlers to find accommodation, work for wages and buy essential goods in the villages of the old inhabitants (*starozhily*) with the cooperation of the village commune (*sel'skoe obshchestvo*). They could also depend on the help of the community (*obshchina*) in the preparation of farming and ploughing their own new plot of land.

Information about the places of settlement was derived from state-sponsored writings on resettlement which appeared in the late 1880s. The Siberian Railway Committee or the Resettlement Administration started disseminating information and issued printed decrees and resettlement-related articles. *Zemstvo* officials published settlement manuals (*putevoditeli*), route maps and itineraries (*marshruti*) and pamphlets that relayed information on resettlement. These were instruction manuals and gave an overview of the environment on which the settlers were encouraged to settle. There was an image of a potentially harsh habitat, or rather an unknown habitat in the east which was also expected to offer genuine possibilities to the settlers. Information also came to the settlers in the form of 'kopeck novels' that depicted eastern regions as places of bounty that were being reached through gigantic railroad projects. Information about village culture in Siberia was screened and passed on by 'village journalists' in the form of peasant folk tales, folk songs, folk myths and folk art. Besides these, there were very little settler writings and settlers' letters recording experiences of settlement and representing first-person accounts about a phenomenon in the late imperial period when there was maximum dispersal of peasant settlements in the eastern borderlands. The experience of travelling by road on the *trakt*, crossing versts of steppe land to reach the destination, i.e. 'good land', was itself a memorable one. The letters reflect the joy of travel and Sunderland makes a wonderful selection of the letters and their writers. The abundance of produce made settlement a memorable issue—in Tomsk, mushrooms were abundant; in Ussuri, oats, rye, hemp, potato, watermelon, cucumber, beans were available in plenty. Siberia to some was a paradise of plenty, others recommended against it. Sunderland's study indicates the range of peasant voices and how resettlement in late imperial Russia opened up as an arena of contact between the settler community and the original inhabitants.[36]

There is thus an overarching enthusiasm to project peasant resettlement as a classic example of frontier development. The emphasis on the role of peasants and their special category status is sometimes counteracted by a series of other assessments. David Moon does not perceive settlement as a concentrated effort of the nineteenth century. By indicating the shifts of settlement over a span of three and a half centuries—from the forest heartland of Muscovy to the south-eastern frontier of the steppe and finally to the eastern territories, Moon was actually suggesting that peasants were *settled and resettled* and the priorities of settlement varied from person to person and from period to period.[37] The idea of taking into consideration the peasant voice was dominant in both Moon and Sunderland's works. Both these studies indicate the inner working of peasant societies. Drawing from the observations of Alfred Crosby and William McNeill about the new environment to which the Russian settlers adapted themselves so readily,[38] Moon argues that settlement conditions in Siberia were far better and that the settlers came from harsher backgrounds (serf status, disease-proneness). This argument while pointing to better living conditions in Siberia, however, does not repudiate the thesis of underlying differences that led to conflicts.[39]

OBLASTNICHESTVO

This was therefore how Siberia was being revealed—as a land of great promise. Unlike earlier images of a frightening landscape that was subject to exploitation, there were refreshing insights about Siberia as Russia's destiny. Emancipated minds became more persuasive about Siberia's economic and cultural development, about Russia's Asia presence which became the essence of patriotic writings of the 1860s. The two outstanding representatives of Siberian patriotism, Nikolai Yadrintsev

(1842-94) and Grigorii Potanin (1834-1920) were the leading *oblastniki* who conceived of Siberia as a regional variant. Their writings have a relevance in the discourse about regionalism that focuses on the *krai* as a vibrant domain. The image of the *oblastniki* as a group of aspirant journalist-writers of Irkutsk who in the 1860s expressed their sentiments for Siberian land and people and which eventually stimulated the aspirations of the autonomists of a post-revolutionary generation has received fairly wide coverage. What is perhaps less emphasized is the fact that *oblastnichestvo* also represented cultural ideals of a group of intellectuals who were a fairly dispersed group in the Russian circuit and also had supporters in Central Asia. *Oblastnichestvo* is idealized as a phenomenon that defined the aspirations of a caucus group of Siberia in which Grigorii Potanin and N.M. Yadrintsev figured as eminent journalists writing in *Vostochnoe Obozrenie* and *Sibirskie Voprosy*. Potanin dealt with the theoretical aspects of the Siberian 'programme' which extended far beyond Siberian regional interests. His ideas were firmly entrenched in the Eastern hypothesis which represented a cultural rationale. According to Potanin, every sociocultural group had the capability of developing autonomously according to its own interests that were linked to its cultural essence. He rejected the theory of evolutionism, the Eurocentric scientific theory that was devoid of the aesthetics of cultural belonging. Potanin represented a mindset that denounced nineteenth-century Eurocentric rationale and was averse to conceptual clichés of intellectual thinking. His philosophy of an eastern inertia was the guiding spirit of his Eastern hypothesis. This became the subject of analysis of the civilizational debate, i.e. the debate about whether Russia civilized her east or whether civilization flowed from the east. According to Potanin, Siberia represented the eastern ideal and was the original homeland of the eastern tribes and was a root trope that fragmented into numerous directions and spread throughout Eurasia. Potanin's views about migration of eastern tribes indicated a radical ideological change in Russia in the nineteenth century.

N.M. Yadrintsev on the other hand was less a philosopher and more a realist. His realism sprang from his association with the administration of west Siberian governor-generalate during 1876-81. He had access to the documents of the state commissions, the decrees and notes issued by the governor-generalate of western Siberia which led to his introspection about the foundations of Russian economic policy, the settlement question, the role of the exiles as well as the aborigines of western Siberia. His in-depth studies, related mostly to the aborigines and the *inorodetsy* phenomenon of Siberia, was the result of several years of his service in western Siberia and his acquaintance with Altai after participating in several expeditions that were led by west Siberian *guberniya*. He represented Siberia as a culturological enigma and was especially enamoured by the ethnographic similarities between the Asian and European cultures. Yadrintsev was enthusiastic about source-study and the uniqueness of his book *Sibir' kak koloniya* (1892) lies in real life depiction of the Minusinsk Basin as the centre of hectic economic activity. The opening up of the Taiga region as an economic space in the 1880s and the special mention of the Tatars of the Tomsk province and the Yenisei *inorodetsy* activity points to his real interest in locating the gaps of methodology of research and unfolding 'missing links' as the nomads made their transition to a settled way of life.

There is immense fascination in Yadrintsev as a historian, economist, ethnographer, linguist and geographer—his manifold expertise gave him the recognition that he deserved. To establish his point about transition, Yadrintsev gave a list of the natural conditions which determined the existence of everyday life. His special reference was to the Altai's natural features that made it a zone of interaction between the Russian peasant settlers and the Altai inhabitants, invigorating the White Tsar legend in the Altai hills.[40] It is the good natural conditions in the Altai that made it a unique case study and a field that was relatively underrepresented. It had an advantageous locale and Yadrintsev was bent on portraying an entire ***raion*** of economic significance.

The most interesting aspect of his works was the ***inorodetsy*** question and the perception of tribal culture. He was enthusiastic about the genealogy of the Siberian tribes and was interested in describing the interrelationship between the Russians and the aborigines not as a set of relations that emerged due to Russian occupation of Siberia, which according to evolutionists meant a decisive break with the past. On the contrary, it was the tribals' adaptation to the environment that was the basis of the Siberian world-view. So, savagery of the aborigines was passé and evolutionism became a field of study. This field, however, had its own limitations and Yadrintsev questioned the premise of evolutionism while addressing the question of the southern nomads (Buryats, Kyrgyzes and Kalmyks).

Yadrintsev, a critic of his own convictions, evolved continuously as a thinker and became an institution by himself. His disciples, belonging to the Russian, Asian and Western academic circuits, adopted his principles and applied them to their realm of studies. Yadrintsev's emphasis on an exclusive tribal environment was reiterated by commentators like L.M. Goryushkin. In his tribute to the legacy of institution-based research in the Soviet Union, Goryushkin, the historian and philologist from Tomsk University recounted milestones in his academic career. He had the training of a Soviet academic but became receptive to new methodologies. His institutional engagements brought him Soviet institutional support to study Russia's borderlands.[41] Goryushkin wrote an introductory chapter on Yadrintsev's book that speaks of Soviet institutions' deep interest in Siberia's aborigines and how these institutions made special use of Yadrintsev's doctrine to promote a Soviet paradigm about aborigines of Siberia as a special category.[42] Their speciality was their dress, the length of their hair, the shape of their noses—all of that became an intrinsic part of a research community that was promoting the idea of Siberia as integral to Russia but distant from the Russians' psyche.[43] Goryushkin's ability to disseminate information about Siberian popular life brought him close to a section of scholars from the Western world.[44]

The appreciation of *oblastnichestvo* as a cultural phenomenon has been undertaken very recently. It opens a gamut of ideas about philosophy and culture that was expressed by the nineteenth century intellectual community of imperial Russia. It is this intellectual community and their writings that had a special angle in Soviet historiography. Soviet historians writing for the five-volume authoritative Soviet account of Siberia, traced the intellectual legacy in Siberia. In characteristic Soviet style, it was pointed out that nineteenth-century intellectuals of Siberia were voicing their sentiments against colonial exploitation of peasants. Colonialism and capitalism were synonymous in Soviet terms and social activists were acting on the guidance of Siberian intellectuals. *Oblastnichestvo* gradually metamorphosed as post-revolutionary euphoria for political autonomy. *Istoriya Sibiri* is endowed with a Marxist interpretation. It reflected on emancipation as an ideal and an entire generation of emancipated minds followed Yadrintsev as their leader. It was the milieu in which Yadrintsev wrote that was highlighted. The 'capitalist epoch' in Siberia was portrayed as inimical to the region's all-round development and historians like L.B. Krasin, Ya. M. Sverdlov, M.K. Vetoshkin wrote on this aspect in regionalist newspapers and journals like *Vostochnoe Obozrenie*.

Yadrintsev inspired an entire generation of writers and his reflections about tribal communities in Siberia were reiterated in ethnographic studies. The 1897 census became the basis of statistical analysis of S. Patkanova in 1906, 1911 and 1912. Yadrintsev was seeking the rehabilitation of the peasantry in Siberia and it is this that brought him close to the line of thinking of the autonomists. The peasant cause became directly related to Soviet preoccupations with the exploiter and the exploited. His idea of an abnormal colonial condition in Siberia whereby the villages were dependent on the metropole had immediate response among activists of his generation. In volumes three and four of *Istoriya Sibiri* we get an idea about how intellectuals were gradually drawn into the politicized atmosphere that was dominated by the SRs.[45] Yadrintsev's rescue mission of 'liberating Siberia from the aggressive currents of capitalist development'[46] had immense appeal among Russian social activists. The mercantilist phenomenon in Siberian cities like Tomsk, Tobolsk and Irkutsk, which was the subject matter of a series of Siberia-centric monographs, was also indicated.[47] The emphasis changed from generation to generation. In the 1920s, the activist networking was widely prevalent in the pronouncements of the *oblastniki*. The peasant cause became a common cause that was directly related to Soviet preoccupations with the exploiter and the exploited. In the post-Second World War period, the emphasis was on socialist reconstruction and historians, geographers and political economists were encouraged to write about regions that got a facelift or regions that had the potential of structural growth. The legacy of *Sibirovedeniya* in Soviet historical studies was highlighted. The critique of colonialism addressed a host of questions of the colonial era. Special attention was given to the settlement question, Stolypin's reforms, the economic transformation of the Yenisei *guberniya*, industrial regeneration, working class movement in western and eastern Siberia, and so on. The history of cities had a wider focus during the period 1949-66. The idea was a display of Soviet Siberia. The national-liberation issue got a new lease of life and the Marxist interpretation was applied to historical-ethnographic sketches of Siberian nationalities. Autonomous republics and *oblasts* (Gornyi Altai, Khakass, Tuva, Buryatia, Yakutia) featured prominently in the subject list. Special attention was given to profiles of activists and academics like A.P. Shchapov who headed the Irkutsk caucus and other 'soyuz' groups in Ekaterinburg, St. Petersburg, Moscow, Kiev as in Omsk, Chita and Perm. Regional publications that reflected on the history, archaeology and ethnography of Siberia, gazettes and journals reflecting the ideas and activities of Siberian Bolsheviks were republished. These included Omsk-based *Stepnovo kraia*, Tomsk-based *Sibirskoi Zhizn'* (Tomsk), Krasnoyarsk-based *Eniseiya* and Irkutsk-based *Vostochnovo Obozreniya* and Blagoveshchensk-based *Amurskovo Kraia*. Siberia-based participation was highlighted more often in historians' conferences and discussion forums. Retrospection about SR's networking among the 'natives' of Siberia indicate apprehension among cadres regarding extension of Bolshevik activism to the Far North. The euphoria about the *zemstvos* and local self-government among the local people created a rift about the land policies that could be implemented. The local people, especially the Buryats too were pressing their own demands about grazing and arable lands which were under threat because of the revolutionary agenda. The Yakuts, an enterprising lot with good educational backgrounds, were aspiring for public posts in preference to the Russians.[48]

Internal rift was central to many of the Soviet-style writings about Siberian activism that represented a complex interplay of separatism, autonomy, regionalism and unitary action. Dina A. Amanzhalova has pointed out that revolutionary transformation in the early twentieth century was an ambiguous process and it was not before October 1917 that debates about a full-scale restructuring on the basis of autonomy took place.[49] The February-October period, according to Amanzhalova, represented a chaotic phase when nationalities were pitched against one another. After October 1917, autonomy was the priority of frontline Siberian *oblastniki*, some of whom had immense faith in *oblastnichestvo* as a 'healthy' expression of patriotism and statehood (*gosudarstvennost'*). The Provisional Siberian government, formed by the *oblastniki* after October 1917, set forth on a new line of action—legitimization of autonomy. Whether there would be national-cultural autonomy first and political autonomy later was an issue that became less and less clear. Amanzhalova's article indicates that Siberian *oblastniki* had good harmless intentions of carrying forth the idea of independent development of Siberia that would be placed under the jurisdiction of a Ministry of Native Affairs which meant that there would be proper legitimization efforts and that the regional projects would not be aimless or haphazard. Amanzhalova's article is couched in the Bolshevik rhetoric of nation-building and laments how a movement for autonomy fell from grace and different interest groups of Siberia, Kazakh Alash, Bashkiria and Turkestan collaborated rather unevenly with each other. Amanzhalova laments that anti-Bolshevik forces played a major role in destabilizing the movement which otherwise showed a lot of promise. Throughout 1918, following the dissolution of the provincial governments and the formulation of the All Russian Provisional Government, there was a concerted effort to make military strength a top priority, which led to further pitfalls like alignments with the White forces and and unrealistic proposition of backing local self-government 'potential' in the Buryat regions of the Irkutsk province and Transbaikal district. The Buryat initiative was soon defamed as 'ethno-political Buryat separatism with a Mongol orientation'.[50]

Like Buryatia, Gornyi Altai also became the pivot of Civil War dissensions. Even after the Bolshevik takeover, the problem of tackling dissenting voices continued and the Narkomnats and Sibrevkom were the institutions of power that were seriously involved in the complex restructuring process that never were resolved to the interest of Siberia. Amanzhalova's critique of the internal cliques that ruined the prospects of *oblastnichestvo* is a sharp contrast to the versions of the apologists of the February Revolution and its principal supporters. Elena Varneck, the Polish ideologue and I.I. Serebrennikov, a key participant during the Civil War ardently felt that the tribal regions of Siberia, especially the Buryats, Altaians and the Kyrgyz demonstrated extraordinary tenacity in carrying forth the *oblastniki's* political agenda. The regional congresses became the platform of representing such tribal interests and Varneck's suggestion was to consider all these trends because they indicated the preparatory phase of multiple alignments. March 1917 saw the early beginnings of alliances between Turkestani nationalists, Alash Ordians, Bashkirs and

Siberian regionalists when the views of ideologues like Shashkov and Yadrintsev were revived as projects for an autonomous Siberia in a Russian federation. The regionalists' involvement in a series of political partnerships with the Socialist Revolutionary groups (SRs) set the stage for future political alliances.

The SR prominence in Siberia, the lack of support for the Bolshevik programme of land seizure by peasants, the demand for an autonomous Siberian socialist republic, contacts with the independent Ukrainian government to explore possibilities of a Russian federation were indications of Siberia blossoming as an independent political unit. The early revolutionary setting in Siberia was as follows: benevolent attitude of the regionalists towards the local tribes that was not acceptable to many members of the workers and peasants' soviets that had established themselves fairly well in the industrial cities of Tomsk, Barnaul and Krasnoyarsk. Vice versa, there was opposition to the revolutionaries—prosperous Russian settlers on the steppe lands south of the Trans-Siberian Railway objected to the Bolshevik policy of grain requisition in order to help the towns. Agricultural communes were not at all helpful for the prosperous farmers who therefore became the principal opponents to the Bolshevik programme. Thus, an important ingredient of Siberian activism was tribal sentiments and Elena Varneck's account is an important testimony to this effect.

Radicalism among Siberians centring the city of Tomsk, the birthplace of Potanin, is reflected in the account of I.I. Serebrennikov. His account unfolds the activity that blossomed in Tomsk surrounding the publishing world. In their daily and monthly periodicals, the Siberian regionalists advocated the extension of *zemstvo* activity to Siberia. The other aspect that received attention was the integration of a dispersed Siberian population that was forced into military service during the First World War. Tomsk's academic circuit and journalists' club were responsive to political decisions that were being enacted on a larger scale in other regions of Siberia and linked it up to Russia's global interests during the period of allied intervention. Serebrennikov's account opens with a regional coverage and subsequently assumes an international character. The spectacle of *oblastnichestvo* in Tomsk and the Irkutsk district is one aspect. Circulation of pamphlets, lectures and proclamations on the regionalist questions became a common occurrence. In Tomsk was drafted the first constitution of the Siberian Regional Duma and it was expected that on the basis of this draft, executive action was to be taken on issues pertaining to land and other questions. The burgeoning activism in Tomsk is a matter that is rarely mentioned in analytical articles about *oblastnichestvo*. Serebrennikov writes about the proceedings of the Siberian Duma amidst the tension that prevailed. The Duma members elected themselves as members of a Provisional Siberian Government and took refuge in Harbin which became the cradle of anti-Bolshevik opposition. The second aspect is internationalism which received a thrust as the autonomous government mustered external support and targeted the Bolshevik centres of control in Omsk, Tomsk, Barnaul, Semipalatinsk and Novosibirsk. The idea was to overpower the Bolsheviks militarily with the help of external support. This takeover was a dramatic episode in the history of the Siberian autonomy movement and challenged the hypothesis of critics that it was failed from the start. Serebrennikov highlights the milestones in the movement for autonomy—the formation of an independent Siberian republic in July 1918 and its brief existence till November 1918 is an underrepresented fact in the history of Siberia. The inauguration of a republic was bound to raise optimism among the people. Despite the fact that the movement came to a blunt end in 1923 and Soviet rule was firmly established all over Siberia, it did arouse a lot of expectation among the aspirants about local self-government. Serebrennikov hoped that this experience would regenerate Russia in general. He certainly was expecting the very best for the Sibiriaks. The positive bent of mind of Serebrennikov is lacking in most of his contemporaries. He was not thinking in terms of immediate political gains but in terms of Russia's diplomatic gains. His version was not tainted by the 'bourgeois tinge' which most of the Bolshevik opponents have been charged with. Yet, he did rely on the international success of *oblastnichestvo*.[51]

The subject of emigration and exile's sentiments is the central theme of a genre of new-age writings in Siberia. Natalia Ablazhei and M.V. Shilovsky have analysed the economic, cultural, social and political contexts of *oblastnichestvo* and bring to light regionalism as a global phenomenon. From their writings it is evident that *oblastnichestvo* is susceptible to varying interpretations. The model of economic federalism has appealed to these writers who have examined varying contours of a centre-periphery relationship. Ablazhei's contention about the progression of *oblastnichestvo* from local particularist sentiments to a federative model emanates from her analysis of the post-revolutionary situation. Since then, especially after the Civil War and the intervention of the Great Powers and the Sibiriaks' emigration to the Far East and Pacific region, the *oblastniki* started interpreting Siberia's destiny in their own ways and the world-view of the *oblastniki* became more pronounced in the post-revolutionary period. N.M. Yadrintsev's nineteenth-century polemic of Siberia as a Russian colony that concentrated on Siberia as a resource hub and a principal supplier of Russia's gold and furs became outdated though it was recognized as the cult doctrine for defining the unequal centre-periphery relations. Gradually, *oblastnichestvo* became a model for cultural diffusion and represented a sophisticated model that went beyond the scope of Darwinism and the evolutionary model.

The new look of *oblastnichestvo* is its association with the intellectuals of Siberia. Though conceived as a lost case in political terms, the movement clearly went beyond the reams of politics. Between the February and the October revolutions, the Siberians did have their own illusions of constitutionalism. But what is also significant is the reaction of several educated groups during the entire period that were advocating neutrality and not actually professing any extreme course of action. This has been the standpoint of another set of emergent literature on *oblastnichestvo* that has dealt with the proliferation of group identities in Siberian cities on the basis of archival source materials as well as materials in private collections.[52]

A MOSAIC OF IMPRESSIONS

Post-Soviet literature thus reflects a mosaic of impressions about Siberia. The relevance of a Russian imperial framework is not the only parameter that has been discussed. Milestones of discovery and conquest are passé. But that does not divert attention from images associated with the imperial core. Such images are not about an expanding zone of political control or the extent of hegemony but also reflect an interest in eastern attributes. A gamut of ideas reveals the intertwined histories of a Eurasian space, reflecting on a series of historical phenomena, a Eurasian spectrum of political upheavals and migratory movements of nomadic tribes, the expansion and contraction of nomadic confederations and the relevance of Andre Gunder Frank's thesis about integrated history and world economy, coalescing regions and time frames that are significant interludes in a historical continuum.[53] With this is challenged the notion of 'centrality' of a Eurasian space that superimposed one administrative centre over many peripheries. The hypothesis of isolation of borderlands has been challenged and the argument has shifted towards a macrohistory with several interrelated and intertwined histories or fragments of history. The historiography of Siberia indicates both continuities and discontinuities. On the one hand, there is an affirmation of Siberia's Russian legacy, the encounter syndrome typified by campaigners like Yermak, that has a large impact on nationalist historiography. On the other hand, there is a deeper understanding of 'the other voice' that romanticizes Siberia's Turko-Mongol heritage, her indigenous traditions and spirituality that were almost not discussed in Soviet annals of history. What we see today are the attributes of a region that is portrayed not as the backyard of the Russian Empire but as a steppe borderland with a living history that needs to be restored from the Russian past. The web of transnational identities is a reality that cannot possibly be overshadowed by the saga of imperial discovery. This aspect has been reviewed by the present generation of intellectuals who are emphatic about the interactive space that Siberia represents.

NOTES

1. The drama, according to Rene Grousset, occurred when the pastoral nomadic people encountered the advanced agriculturist neighbours of Eurasia, i.e. the sedentary peoples of China, Iran and Europe to whom the Mongols, Huns and the Turkomans were savages indeed. Rene Grousset, *The Empire of the Steppes: A History of Central Asia*, tr. from French by Naomi Walford, London: Rutgers University Press, 1970, Preface, p. viii.
2. Reuven Amitai and Michael Biran, scholars in Israel, have taken the initiative of reviving the nomadic component of Eurasia. Reuven Amitai and Michael Biran (eds.), *Mongols, Turks and Others: Eurasian Nomads and the Sedentary World*, Leiden: Brill, 2005.
3. Stephen Kotkin, 'Introduction—Rediscovering Russia in Asia', in Stephen Kotkin and David Wolff (eds.), *Rediscovering Russia in Asia: Siberia and the Russian Far East*, Armonk: M.E. Sharpe, 1995, p. 3. James Forsyth however makes a distinction between 'Siberia discovered' and 'Siberia invaded', pointing to commercial ventures that preceded the actual conquests. James Forsyth, *A History of the Peoples of Siberia: Russia's North Asian Colony, 1581-1990*, Cambridge: Cambridge University Press, 1994 (paperback edition), chapters 1 and 2.
4. Catherine the Great's convictions about Siberia as the source of imperial grandeur was replaced by cynicism in the early nineteenth century and the declining importance of the fur trade led to a role-reversal, i.e. Siberia as land of exile, dank and barren land with gloomy penal mines. There was another change of status after the Decembrist uprising in 1825 and to the exiles Siberia represented freedom. It was the counter example of what European Russia represented in the early nineteenth century—bonded slavery, powerful landed aristocracy. Therefore, Siberia got a facelift in the Decembrists' portrayal of unfettered freedom and Siberia was the source of salvation.
5. Erich Kasten (ed.), *Pathways to Reform in Post-Soviet Siberia*, vol. 2 *Properties as Culture—Culture as Property*, Berlin: Dietrich Reimar Verlag, 2005.
6. Eric Newby, *The Big Red Train Ride*, London: Picador, 1978.

7. Websites about Siberian travel are full of descriptions about the 'fantastic journey' from the east to the west that connects the Trans Sib's mainline with the chord lines and passes through Beijing, the Gobi, Ulan Bator, Irkutsk and finally reaches Moscow. http://www.trans-siberia.com.
8. Robert Joseph Kerner, 'The Russian Eastward Movement: Some Observations on its Historical Significance', *Pacific Historical Review*, vol. XVII, no. 2, May 1948.
9. Henry Trofimenko, 'Long-term Trends in the Asia-Pacific Region: A Soviet Evaluation', *Asian Survey*, vol. 29, no. 3, March 1989, p. 239.
10. J.R. Hughes, 'The Irkutsk Affair: Stalin, Siberian Politics and the End', *Soviet Studies*, vol. 41, no. 2, April 1989, p. 231.
11. The *guberniya's* fundamental rearrangement of industrial geography was brought to effect after the completion of the Trans-Siberian Railroad which stimulated population migration to the *guberniya*. Richard E. Lonsdale, 'Siberian Industry Before 1917: The Example of Tomsk Guberniya', *Annals of the Association of American Geographers*, vol. 53, no. 4, December 1963.
12. V. Ya. Tkachenko and B.P. Pertsev, *Sukhoputnyi transport Sibiri: formirivanie opornoi seti zheleznykh I avtomobil'nykh dorog*, Novosibirsk: Institut Istorii SO RAN, 2003.
13. Kimitaka Matsuzato, Preface to 'Emerging Meso-Areas in the Former Socialist Countries: Histories Revived or Improvised?', Twenty-First Century COE Program *Making a Discipline of Slavic Eurasian Studies: Meso-Areas and Globalization*, Sapporo: Slavic Research Center, Hokkaido University, 2005, pp. 7-12.
14. Anatole G. Mazour, *The Writing of History in the Soviet Union*, Stanford: Hoover Institution Press, 1971, p. xii.
15. *Lichnost' v istorii Sibiri, XVIII-XX vekov*, Novosibirsk, 2007; V.A. Skubnevskii and Iu. M. Goncharov, 'Siberian Merchants in the Latter Half of the Nineteenth Century', *Sibirica*, vol. 2, no. 1, April 2002.
16. Igor V. Naumov, *The History of Siberia* (ed. David N. Collins), London: Routledge, 2006, p. 53.
17. James Forsyth, *A History of the Peoples of Siberia: Russia's North Asian Colony 1581-1990*, Cambridge: Cambridge University Press, 1992, p. 29.
18. In Lamb's serial stories about Cossack raiders, we get acquainted with the wolf-like character Khlit, a Cossack raider managing a stronghold in the wide steppe between the Don and the Dneiper. Harold Lamb, *Wolf of the Steppe: The Complete Cossack Adventures* (ed. Howard Andrew Jones), Lincoln: University of Nebraska, 2006.
19. The idea of Cossack military energy in Siberia is, however, open to question. According to recent appraisals of Cossack history, the governance of the *voevodas* was continually changing and the pattern of governance in one fortress town (like Tobolsk) differed from patterns

in other towns. Sometimes, the Cossacks performed as a collective. There is evidence of a 'Cossack public sphere' in juxtaposition to the Muscovite sovereign's 'affair'. Christoph Witzenrath, *Cossacks and the Russian Empire, 1598-1725: Manipulation, Rebellion and Expansion into Siberia*, London: Routledge, 2007, see chapter 'Integration of the Trading Frontier: The Sovereign's Affair', pp. 85-121.

20. *Istoriya Sibiri', s drevneishikh vremen do nashikh dnei, v piati tomakh*, Tom Vtoroi (*Sibir' v sostave feodalnoi Rossii*), Leningrad: Nauka, 1968.
21. The details of the expedition, enumerated in the Stroganov Chronicle, are provided in Terence Armstrong (ed.), *Yermak's Campaign of Siberia: A Selection of Documents Translated from the Russian by Tatiana Minorsky*, London: Haklyut Society, 1975, pp. 35-61.
22. Descriptions from all the three chronicles provide information about the unequal encounter. Kuchum's men were unable with their arrows and spears to destroy the Cossacks who were armed with small shotguns and fortress guns and used small boats to move up and down the rivers. The adversaries were deserted by 'friends' like the Ostyak prince. His favourite, his own son Mametkul, was badly wounded in the battle. Also, there are illustrations about the Cossack encampments along the rivers.
23. *Entsiklopedia Kazachestva*, collection of articles by G.V. Guvarev and A.E. Skrilov, compiled by O.O. Antropov, Moscow: Veche, 2007.
24. Mark Bassin, 'The Russian Geographical Society, the "Amur Epoch", and the Great Siberian Expedition 1855-1863', *Annals of the Association of American Geographers*, 73 (2), 1983, pp. 240-56.
25. Steven G. Marks, *Road to Power: The Trans-Siberian Railroad and the Colonization of Asian Russia*, Ithaca: Cornell University Press, 1991.
26. Debates continued over the direction of the rail routes—northern or southern. First, there was an acceptance of the southern line that was to proceed through major mining centres via Moscow, Nizhnii Novgorod, Kazan, Ekaterinburg and finally be linked with a railroad from the Volga River to the Amur. Subsequently, there were improvements in the financial conditions and the railroad network was conceived of in a big way—extending up to Orenburg, at the southwestern border of Siberia. Thus, it was not until the 1880s that the notion of a railroad that would run through Siberia was planned. The finally planned route bypassed the original southern route and was revised as follows: from Samara on the Volga to Ufa, then to Zlatoust in the Urals, whence it would emerge at Cheliabinsk and continue through western Siberia to Omsk. The next stage would be to pass from Omsk to Krasnoyarsk and Irkutsk. A post road through Chita along the Amur River would reach Khabarovsk and then would turn south along the Ussuri River to Vladivostok. The reason why this route became more popular than the rest was because of the fact that the

Samara-Ufa connector ran through the centre of the Siberian Black Earth Zone that lay close to regions where coal and livestock were in plenty. Marks, op. cit.

27. Claudia Weiss, 'Representing the Empire: The Meaning of Siberia for Russian Imperial Identity', *Nationalities Papers*, 35, no. 3 (July 2007), p. 439.
28. Anindita Banerjee, 'The Trans-Siberian Railroad and Russia's Asia: Literature, Geopolitics, Philosophy of History', *Clio*, 34, 1: 2, 2004-5.
29. Inga Tsupenkova, *A.P. Chekov v kulturnom prostrantsve Dal'nevo Vostoka Rossii v kontse XX-nachale XXI veki*, in Mochizuki Tetsuo (ed.), *Chekov and Stalin: Siberia and the Russian Far East in the 21st Century: Partners in the "Community of Asia"*, Hokkaido: Slavic Research Center, 2005.
30. Eric Newby, *The Big Red Train Ride*, London: Picador, 1978, pp. 120-1.
31. Donald Treadgold, *The Great Siberian Migration*, Princeton: Princeton University Press, 1957, which is a classic on the narrative of migration; Leonid M. Goryushkin, 'Migration, Settlement and the Rural Economy of Siberia, 1861-1914', in Alan Wood (ed.), *The History of Siberia: From Russian Conquest to Revolution*, London: Routledge, 1991; David Moon, 'Peasant Migration and the Settlement of Russia's Frontiers, 1550-1897', *The Historical Journal*, 40 (4), 1997.
32. According to studies, there were 35,000 peasant migrants per year in the 1880s which rose to approximately 96,000 per year in the late 1890s and became a flood in the period between 1906-14 (i.e. after P.A. Stolypin legalized the peasant movement). Forsyth, op. cit., p. 191.
33. Moon, op. cit., p. 863.
34. There was intra-community tension. The new settlers clashed with the old Siberians, especially in the mining (gold) operations. Also, the bustling middle class that came into prominence as part of the development programme was not liked by the original settlers and communities. Forsyth, op. cit., p. 197.
35. Goryushkin, op. cit., pp. 141-2.
36. William Sunderland, 'Peasant Pioneering: Russian Peasant Settlers Describe Colonization and the Eastern Frontier, 1880s-1910', *Journal of Social History*, vol. 34, no. 4, Summer 2001.
37. Moon, op. cit.
38. Willian H. McNeill, *Plagues and Peoples*, New York: Anchor Books, 1976; Alfred W. Crosby, *Ecological Imperialism: The Biological Expansion of Europe, 900-1900*, Cambridge: Cambridge University Press, 1986, 1993.
39. Conflicts mostly arose out of the crucial issue of land. The lifestyles were different and the associated economic, social and political systems

entailed radically different ways of using the land and concepts of landownership. From the late sixteenth century, the Russian state expropriated nomads' pastures and handed them out to Russian settlers and simply permitted Russian migrants to take land for themselves. In many regions incoming migrants bargained with the local people who had no idea about buying or renting of land and scant understanding what the deals meant or what they were offered in return.

40. L.M. Goryushkin, 'Glavniy trud N.M. Yadrintseva', in *Sibir' kak koloniya v geograficheskom, etnograficheskom I istoricheskom otnoshenii*, of the series *Istoriya istochniki: pervoistochniki*, Vypusk III, Novosibirsk, 2003, pp. 15-16.
41. Among the works that he reviewed were institutional publications of the Soviet period (especially of the Institute of Ethnography of Academy of Sciences) including fascinating surveys about non-Russian aborigines by G.M. Davidov and the local tribal settings of the Trans-Baikal region as well as of Yakutia, Polar region and the Yenisei basin—works that continued the nineteenth-century intellectual tradition of studying Siberia as a unique setting. To pay tribute to their master's range of thoughts, Novosibirsk's historians have brought out a collection of commentaries on Yadrintsev's legendary work and Goryushkin was one of the outstanding commentators of the Soviet period.
42. L.M. Goryushkin, 'Glavniy trud N.M. Yadrintseva', in *Sibir' kak koloniya v geograficheskom, etnograficheskom I istoricheskom otnoshenii*, of the series *Istoriya istochniki: pervoistochniki*, Vypusk III, Novosibirsk, 2003, p. 20.
43. Ibid.
44. Alan Wood in his obituary about Leonid Mikhailovich Goryushkin (1927-1999), *Sibirica*, vol. 2, no. 1, April 2002, pp. 9-10.
45. *Istoriya Sibir', s drevneishikh vremen do nashikh dnei v piati tomakh*, Leningrad: Nauka, 1968.
46. *Vostochnoe Obozrenie* (1896).
47. Works cited are: K. Golodnikov, 'Gorod Tobol'sk i evo okrestnosti', *Istoricheski ocherk*, Tobolsk, 1886; K. Golodnikov, *Ekonomicheskiesostanie gorodskikh poselenii Sibirii*, SPB, 1882; A.V. Andrijanov, *Tomsk v proshlom I nastoyaschem*, Tomsk, 1890; *Gorod Tomsk*, 1912, etc.
48. Elena Varneck, 'Siberian Native Peoples after the February Revolution', *Slavonic and East European Review*, vol. 2, no. 1, March 1943.
49. Dina A. Amanzhalova, 'The Movement for Siberian Regional and National Autonomy in the Early 1920s', *Sibirica*, vol. 3, no. 1, 2003.
50. Russian archival documents of GARF as quoted by Amanzhalova, op. cit., p. 93.
51. I.I. Serebrennikov, 'The Siberian Autonomous Movement and its Future', *The Pacific Historical Review*, vol. 3, no. 4, December 1934.

52. The source that has been cited specially is S.A. Krasil'nikov and V.L. Soskin, *Intelligentsia Sibiri v period borby za pobedu I utverzhdenie Sovetskoi vlasti (1917-leto 1918)*. See review of the book by Patrick R. Taylor in *The American Historical Review*, vol. 92, no. 4, October 1987, p. 1009.
53. Andre Gunder Frank, *ReOrient: Global Economy in the Asian Age*, Berkeley and Los Angeles, California: University of California Press, 1998.

CHAPTER 4

Epilogue

TRENDS

In the last 15-20 years, scholarship on the Eurasian steppe, especially its nomadic environment has increased considerably. The urge to study the steppe history in long duree has not waned and specialists have followed Rene Grousset's methodology of examining the steppe through the lens of dynastic and military upheavals stretching from Hungary to Manchuria. Grousset's work clearly set the trend of examining the nomadic bastion and there was overwhelming attention to the millennia-old nomadic history and the 500-year span of nomadic tutelage and the clash and combination of economic interests of the 'barbarian' and the 'civilized', demonstrated by the Cambridge researchers on early Inner Asia.[1] The profile of a sedentary-nomadic interactive space has set the tone of writings in the contemporary period. In this context, Owen Lattimore's conceptual framework of Chinese borderlands has been revived, leading to fresh assessments about the frontier and borderland as a tool of historical analysis. In the present study, I have tried to work within this framework, taking into consideration the multiple dimensions of a steppe environment, loosely described as nomadic and implying a political sphere of control but connoting a human environment that Lattimore had described and what his disciple David Christian had reiterated.[2] The gaze has thus shifted decisively to the nomadic domain and the durable features of nomadic economy, and the forms of pastoral nomadism in south and east of Russia are discussed more often.[3]

But these works mostly describe the early history of the steppe and its broad geographical space as well as the prevalence of Turkic, Mongol and Persian lineages. The strong influence of historical geography, a discipline that was claimed to have been revived in the 1980s by British writers like James H. Bater and R.A. French, is felt. Scattered writings on the Eurasian steppe sometimes reflect a bias—the bias is about the empire and the magnitude of its extent, sometimes leaving out the steppe locale and its overlapping territories.

Soviet and post-Soviet approaches are extremely diverse. Soviet history projects were grand-scale ethnicity-centric studies that hardly took into account steppe reactions among the Kalmyks, Buryats and the Cossacks. Post-Soviet writings have gone the other way and have examined disruptions in the empire's fabric or have highlighted unrepresented facts. While the Soviet material is rigid and follows the Communist Party line, a bulk of the post-Soviet material is scattered and touches upon an array of subjects. A section of post-Soviet writings focus on the Volga-Tatars, the Bashkirs, the Chuvash and the Maris. The others have tried to showcase Cossack heroism, Siberian nationalism and Chingizid legacy.

Against this background, I began a random selection of literature that are relevant to the steppe cosmos and finally restricted myself to a limited subject: representation of steppe history. I principally concentrated upon diverse opinions during the Soviet and post-Soviet periods. On the one hand, there have been opinions about 'empire' as a category[4] and multiple concerns about frontiers and borderlands. On the other hand, there has been a sort of local knowledge, reflected through what the sociologists saw at the local level. The dual impressions have rendered an understanding about the ways in which the steppe was represented: (a) as a periphery of the Russian empire that was turbulent and unforgiving, (b) as an integrative space and human environment that was lenient and accommodating.

CONTENT ANALYSIS

For the purpose of the present study, I focused on frontier studies, its evolution as a history of ideas ever since Frederick Jackson Turner and Owen Lattimore propounded their views about the American and Inner Asian frontiers, respectively. The new literature on frontier contacts urged me to consider contemporary images about the Siberian frontier and Central Asian borderlands that overlap with Xinjiang and Mongolia. The 'Russia in Asia' paradigm of Stephen Kotkin and David Wolff that deals with Russia's presence in Asian borderlands is a useful starter. From the wide range of Soviet and post-Soviet opinions on Eurasia, I tried to deduce a picture of the steppe as an interactive space. The literature that was available sometimes did not exclusively describe the steppe developments, but did provide an understanding of the patterns of writing that were related to Russia's southern and eastern fringe and Inner Asia.

The study progresses from an analysis of Grousset's description of dynastic regimes in the steppe to local studies about Horde groupings in the southern and eastern fringes of the Russian empire, the prominence of Turkic interest groups in the western steppe region, the proliferation of heroic legacies to nineteenth-century developments describing ambiguous relationships about land and the essence of Kazakh activism and regional aspirations among the Siberians. Grousset's impressions about Attila the Hun's expansion to the West may not seem out of place in a large chronological span that deals with West to East dynastic upheavals and migratory movements. The implication of Grousset's argument is that Hunnic raids determined the fate of empires in Eurasia. An alternative argument of Reuven Amitai and Michael Biran, however, suggests that it were the Mongols who established a trend of governance, institution-building and exchange system that brought them into close contact with their sedentary neighbours. Amitai, Biran, Kotkin and Morgan, though inspired by the chronological span that Grousset introduces, are more emphatic about the inner strength of the Mongols and their nomadic pastoral economy that urges them to move from place to place in search of pastures and water for their horses but never dislocate them from the terrain. This makes their polities more durable than one can possibly imagine. Though the nomadic parameter is repeatedly addressed, it is not the only feature in steppe historiography of the twentieth century. Soviet writings on the steppe were focused on the 'feudal' aspect of the local regimes whereas in the post-Soviet period, there has been an attempt to focus on the hegemony of the local Khans who asserted their land rights at various stages. Such divergent approaches indicate growing appreciation for a dynamic locale that was not merely responding as a military fortress of the imperial administration but also reflecting its own energy as a provincial commercial enclave and entrepôt of trade that had sizeable commercial contacts (e.g. Minusinsk basin in the Yenisei *guberniya*) and as an intellectual repository with Semipalatinsk and Irkutsk as the nerve centres. The legacy of a people's history in Kazakhstan takes the discussion to a new level.

The discussion is also about the new framework of Siberian history. The dominant narrative about colonial transformation (through the railroad venture and peasant resettlement programme) is juxtaposed to competing narratives about the spatial identity of a 'region'—an idea that became the credo of the autonomy movement of the *oblastniki* in the early twentieth century. On the one hand, the dominant narrative highlighted 'discovery' as 'development' that began with Russian contacts in the sixteenth century and culminated in the military reconfiguration of a territory through a network of *streltsy* and *voevodas*. On the other hand, the writings of Grigorii Potanin and N.M. Yadrintsev have secured a place in the discourse about regionalism that focuses on the *krai* as a vibrant domain. The image of the *oblastniki* as a group of aspirant journalist-writers of Irkutsk who in the 1860s expressed their sentiments for Siberian land and people and which eventually stimulated the aspirations of the autonomists of a post-revolutionary generation has received fairly wide coverage. Siberia's 'human environment' too has received a fresh impetus and indigenous communities (Yakuts, Buryat Mongols, Telengit Altaians and the Chukchis) and community traditions considered to be fringe areas in terms of research and subsumed within the overall fabric of development that was showcased by the Soviets have been readdressed by sociologists with a fresh perspective about 'indigeneity'.

This brings me to the multidisciplinary nature of steppe studies. Sociology has come closer to historical studies and vice versa. During the Soviet period, the authorities were attentive to the sociological perspective but their prime concern was *etnos* which implied a social organization. During the Soviet period, the Communist Party 'disciplined' history and the historians were 'instructed' to write within a set framework, e.g. Communist Party's 'revolutionary role'. Within this set-up, the state academies patronized people and institutions and also sponsored projects that dealt with primary sources. Sources were idealized within the framework of *istochnikovedeniya* and in the realm of Siberian studies, the use of sources has received emphasis. Memoirs for instance are an excellent source material about the context of a particular historical event. Novosibirsk's Institute of History journal *Gumanitarnye Nauki v Sibiri* points to the relevance of pre-revolutionary and post-revolutionary memoirs as evidence of the social milieu.[5] Memoirs have an importance in the source-based research of the Siberians. Siberia's historians have pointed to the earnest patronage of memoirs and their preservation by the Soviets. The dissemination of ideas through memoirs is a subject that has derived a lot of attention as a sociocultural phenomenon.[6] Siberian studies are therefore not limited to the historical details of a colonial framework. The present study is also attentive to the 'ground analysis' of Siberia that is an interesting feature of sociological studies. Such ground analysis indicates a greater interest in the diversity of lifestyles, which tends to be the basis of the discussions about the new framework of *sotsial'no-kulturnaia antropologiia* instead of Soviet-style *etnografiya*. Joachim Otto Habeck, a sociologist who is engaged in the study of the urban complex of the Komi Republic, has indicated the new frame of sociological studies of Eurasia:

> It is time to look beyond 'the ethnic' and examine other dimensions of human life and cultural diversity. I would add that it is important to apprehend such concepts as ethnicity, way of life or tradition not merely as 'given' but through the interpretation of the objects of study themselves. I am pleading not simply for the deconstruction of such concepts but rather for the examination of how actors 'in the field' perform and more or less creatively employ such concepts (among which is identity).[7]

QUESTIONS RAISED

The general approach is to raise questions within an imperial framework and specific instances have been cited to explain what the frontier disposition was all about. So, besides a Russia-centric image, there are ideas about a Mongol *mysl*, fragmentary tribal groupings under 'horde' leadership, a loose Turkic confederacy and kaganate strongholds in the western steppe, Chinese military control around the Tarim Basin, the 'conscience' of reformed Kazakh intellectuals, revolutionary activism in Siberia and Kazakhstan in the twentieth century and fractures within the framewok of Siberian regionalism and Alash Orda political activism. The frontier character is also revealed by the profile of Cossackdom, representing the Cossacks as a military category.

The three basic premises that have been questioned in this study are:

(a) *The Eurasian steppe as 'periphery' in the overall colonial framework:* On the contrary, the frontier is considered to be a tool of historical analysis. Contemporary attention has shifted to the individual roles that frontiers played as integral components of an expansionist empire. On the one hand they emerged as a competitive force *vis-à-vis* the colonial settlers. Frontiers also have specificities that make them distinct from one another. They also have economic, social and cultural contacts with each other. Referring to Russia's dynamic southern and eastern borderlands (comprising Kazakhs, Kalmyks and Tatars of the Golden Horde or the Nogai tribe), Andreas Kappeler argues that the steppe frontier of Russia evolved since the sixteenth century from an 'extractive frontier' in western Siberia close to the Urals (where exploitation took place) to a 'settlement frontier' beyond the Urals and south Siberia (where Kazakhs were inducted into Russian military service).

(b) *The ethnic trajectory in the post-disintegration period*: Questions have been raised about the 'primacy of the ethnic' trajectory. The *etnos*, conceptualized in the 1920s, had emerged as a solid concept in the 1970s and the 1980s under the guidance of Yu Bromlei. Sociologists today have questioned this framework of 'ethnic identity' because it has little scope for *individual* preferences. This questioning is particularly relevant to the post-Soviet situation in Kazakhstan where a drive for Kazakhstan stressed on ethnic Kazakhs' differences with their Slavic co-ethnics, especially the Russians. Not many scholars shared Valery Tishkov's prejudiced view about the Kazakh mind and there seems to have been yearnings for a peaceful urban life, especially because the Russians shared a good deal of urban space with the Kazakhs and the Slavic population was engaged in service-oriented professions in Kazakhstan. Also, identifying a *zhuz*-oriented Kazakh political tradition was a futile exercise because heterogeneities already existed in the Turko-Mongol political confederation in the seventeenth and eighteenth centuries that largely influenced *zhuz* affiliations.

(c) *Siberia as wilderness*: Siberia is no longer considered to be an elusive country beyond the Urals where exiles and notorious criminals operated through their own nexus. Such a perspective indicates a flexible stance rather than a rigid overview of a vast unwieldy space. The image of the region as a continental landmass that constituted the core of a rapidly expanding imperial system has also been taken into consideration. The new gaze of area specialists has extended beyond the Siberia's image as Russia's 'extractive frontier' that attracted fur-traders, missionaries, migrants, colonists and intellectuals to a space that had acquired a certain artistic image. This leads to the polemical debate about the 'paradise' that Siberia represents. Siberia's vibrant ecosystem has become the showpiece of Eurasia's environmental diversity and habitat. Siberia's energy sector concentrated in Russia's far east tends to be the focal point of regional studies that deal with parameters of eastward integration and issues of Russian federalism.

FUTURE DIRECTIONS

One might take this study a bit further by exploring the intertwined histories of the steppe. The implication of this study so far is that the Eurasian steppe cannot be studied in a single monochromatic Russian framework. What needs to be explored is how other empires (the Chinese and the Dzhungar) too became similarly engaged in a competition for the heartlands of Eurasia or how the empire was also represented by a confederation of tribal interests as in the case of the Mongols or the Turks. A re-envisioning of Eurasia leads to a search for the antecedents of Eurasianism, that was not exclusive to the Tsarist or Soviet regimes, but also had a pre-Tsarist Mongol setting—a claim that is made by Russia's federal subjects, i.e. Tatarstan, Altai, Buryatiya, Sakha-Yakutia, Kalmykia and others. So what we now have is a matrix of identities built around Tatar and Mongol empires and around legacies of the Golden Horde. With such reconstructed images of the empire and its eastern attributes, one is tempted to study the profile of Eurasia, its imperial configurations, and its pre-imperial political dispensation that has moved away considerably from Russia-centric imperial narratives about development and encounter. The study also needs to be situated in its contemporary framework. The regional affinities and differences can be explored in terms of border alignments, trans-border migration flows, paranoia of Chinese migration and other issues that have appeared within the rubric of new assessments.

NOTES

1. Denis Sinor (ed.), *The Cambridge History of Early Inner Asia*, Cambridge: Cambridge University Press, 1990.
2. David Christian, *A History of Russia, Central Asia and Mongolia: Inner Eurasia from Prehistory to the Mongol Empire*, vol. I, Oxford: Blackwell Publishing, 1998.
3. Works of Anatoly Khazanov, Morris Rossabi, Nicolo Di Cosmo, Reuven Amitai and Michael Biran and Peter Finke indicate the volume of scholarship on the subject of nomadism in the steppe.
4. In a recent study, it has been shown that empires acquired a pattern of behaviour. The Russian empire became a reference point for studying the vicissitudes that determined the character of the imperial state. The character of the Russian empire was affected by conquest-related developments and centripetal forces that accentuated the empire's 'Russian' quality. Hari Shankar Vasudevan, 'Russian Emperialism: The Russian Empire, the Soviet State and the Uncertain Fate of "Empire" in Modern Times', in Jyoti Bhusan Das Gupta (ed.), *Science, Technology, Imperialism and War*, vol. XV, part I, *History of Science, Philosophy and Culture in Indian Civilization*, Centre for Studies in Civilizations, Pearson Longman, 2009.
5. N.P. Matkhanova, 'Sibirskaia memuaristika pervoi poloviny XIX veka kak sotsiokulturny fenomen', *Gumanitarnye Nauki v Sibiri*, no. 3, 2005.
6. *Sibirskie Memuary*, special issue of electronic journal *Sibirskaia Zaimka*, no. 2, 2002, compiled articles that are devoted to Yermak's campaign trail, the White Army in Siberia, dissident literature of the 1980s, and so on.
7. Joachim Otto Habeck, 'Dimensions of Identity' in Erich Kasten (ed.), *Rebuilding Identities: Pathways to Reform in Post-Soviet Siberia*, Berlin: Dietrich Reimer Verlag, vol. 3, 2005, p. 12.

Bibliography

PRIMARY SOURCES

I. Books, Addresses, Essays, Travel Writings

Atkinson, Thomas Witlam. *Oriental and Western Siberia: A Narrative of Seven Years Explorations and Adventures in Siberia, Mongolia, the Kirghiz Steppes, Chinese Tartary and Part of Central Asia*, Philadelphia: J.W. Bradley, 1859 [reprinted by Asian Educational Services, New Delhi, 2000].

Czaplicka, M.A. *Collected Works of M.A. Czaplicka*, ed. David N. Collins, 4 vols., Surrey: Curzon, 1999.

Lattimore, Owen. *Inner Asian Frontiers of China*, The American Geographical Society, 1940. [Republished with the addition of an introduction, Hong Kong: Oxford University Press, 1988.]

——. *Studies in Frontier History: Collected Papers, 1928-1958*, London: Oxford University Press, 1962.

Nansen, Fridtjof. *Siberia: The Land of the Future*, tr. Arthur G. Chater [republished as *Siberian Discovery Series*, ed. David N. Collins, vol. 4], The Quadrant, Richmond: Curzon, 2000.

Price, M.P. *Siberia*, London: Methuen, 1912 [republished as *Siberian Discovery Series*, ed. David N. Collins, vol. 6], The Quadrant, Richmond: Curzon, 2000.

Roerich, Nicholas. *Heart of Asia*, Varanasi: Pilgrims Publishing, 2007.

——. *Altai-Himalaya (A Travel Diary)*, Delhi: Book Faith India, 1929 (republished in 1996).

Sankrityayana, Rahul. *Meri Jeevan Yatra*, tr. into Bengali as *Amar Jibon Jatra*, ed. Satish Mitra and Saikat Rakshit, Rahul

Sankrityayana Birth Centenary Committee, 5 vols, Calcutta, 1995.

Turner, Frederick Jackson. 'The Significance of the Frontier in American History', republished in 1920.

Valikanof, Captain, Veniukof, M. and other Russian travellers, *The Russians in Central Asia: Their Occupation of the Kyrgyz Steppe and the Line of the Syr Darya: Their Political Relations with Khiva, Bokhara and Kokan, also Descriptions of Chinese Turkestan and Dzhungaria* (tr. from the Russian by John and Robert Michell), London: Edward Stanford, 1865.

Zenzinov, Vladimir. *The Road to Oblivion* [republished as *Siberian Discovery Series*, ed. David N. Collins, vol. 11], The Quadrant, Richmond: Curzon, 2000.

II. Directories, Encyclopedias, Official Histories

Borgatta, Edgar F. and Rhonda J.V. Montgomery (eds), *Encyclopedia of Sociology*, vol. 1, Macmillan Reference USA, 2000.

Entsiklopedia Kazachestva, sostavitel' G.V. Gubarev, redactor-izdatel' A.E. Skrilov, Moscow: Veche, 2007.

Entsiklopediceskii Slovar, Leipzig: Brockhauz and Efron, 1890-1907.

Istoriya Sibiri', s drevneishikh vremen do nashikh dnei, v piati tomakh, Leningrad: Nauka, 1968.

Masanov, N.E. et al., *Istoriya Kazakhstana, narody i kultury*, Almaty: Daik Press, 2001.

Russkii Biograficheski Slovar', SPB: Izdetel'stvo Impertorskovo Russkovo Istoricheskovo Obshchestva, 1896-1916.

Viatkin, M. *Ocherki po istorii Kazakhskoi SSSR do drevneishykh vremen po 1870 gody*, Tom pervyi, Ogiz Gospolitizdat, 1941.

SECONDARY SOURCES

I. Books

In English

Amitai, Reuven and Michael Biran (eds.), *Mongols, Turks and Others: Eurasian Nomads and the Sedentary World*, Leiden: Brill, 2005.

Armstrong, Terence. *Yermak's Campaign of Siberia: A Selection of Documents Translated from the Russian by Tatiana Minorsky*, London: Haklyut Society, 1975.

Auezov, Mukhtar. *Abai* (Abridged version), Moscow: Progress Publishers, 1975.

Baddley, John F. *The Ragged Flanks of the Caucasus*, 2 vols, London: Oxford University Press, 1940.

——. *The Russian Conquest of the Caucasus*, London: Longmans, Green, 1940.

Banerji, Arup. *Making the Past Work: Writing History in the Soviet Union*, New Delhi: Social Science Press, 2008.

Barfield, Thomas J. *The Nomadic Alternative*, Englewood Cliffs, NJ: Prentic Hall, 1993.

——. *The Perilous Frontier: Nomadic Empires and China, 221 B.C. to A.D. 1757, Studies in Social Discontinuity*, Cambridge, Massachusetts and Oxford: Blackwell, 1989.

Bassin, Mark. *Imperial Vision: Nationalist Imagination and Geographical Expansion in the Russian Far East, 1840-1865*, Cambridge: Cambridge University Press, 1999.

Beyfogle, Nicholas, Abby Schrader and Willard Sunderland (eds.), *Peopling the Periphery: Slavic Settlement from Muscovite to Soviet Times*, London: Routledge/Curzon, 2007.

Brzezinski, Z. *The Geostrategic Triad: Living with China, Europe and Russia*, Washington: The CSIS Press, 2002.

Brower, Daniel R. and Edward Lazzerini, *The Russian Orient: Imperial Borderlands and Peoples, 1750-1917*, Bloomington: I.B. Tauris, 1997.

Christian, David. *A History of Russia, Central Asia and Mongolia: Inner Eurasia from Prehistory to the Mongol Empire*, vol. I, Oxford: Blackwell Publishing, 1998.

Chivilikhin, Vladimir. *Wilderness Survey: True Story of a Taiga Tragedy*, Moscow: Progress Publishers (date of publication not printed in the book).

Cosmo, Nicola Di. *Ancient China and its Enemies: The Role of Nomadic Power in East Asian History*, Cambridge: Cambridge University Press, 2002.

Crews, Robert D. *For Prophet and Tsar: Islam and Empire in Russia and Central Asia*, Cambridge, Massachusetts: Harvard University Press, 2006.

Crosby, Alfred. *Ecological Imperialism: The Biological Expansion of Europe, 900-1900*, Cambridge: Cambridge University Press, 1993.

Dave, Bhavna. *Kazakhstan: Ethnicity, Language and Power,* London: Routledge/Curzon, 2007.

Dudoignon, Stephane A. and Hisao Komatsu (eds.), *Islam in Politics in Russia and Central Asia (Early Eighteenth to Late Twentieth Centuries)*, London: Kegan Paul International, 2001.

Forsyth, James. *A History of the Peoples of Siberia: Russia's North Asian Colony 1581-1990*, Cambridge: Cambridge University Press, 1992.

Frank, Allen J. *Popular Islamic Literature in Kazakhstan: An Annotated Bibliography*, Hyattsville: Dunwoody Press, 2007.

——. *Muslim Religious Institutions in Imperial Russia: The Islamic World of Novouzensk District and the Kazakh Inner Horde, 1780-1910*, Leiden: Brill, 2001.

Geraci, Robert. *Window on the East: National and Imperial Identities in Late Tsarist Russia*, Ithaca and London: Cornell University Press, 2001.

Grousset, Rene. *The Empire of the Steppes: A History of Central Asia*, tr. from French by Naomi Walford, London: Rutgers University Press, 1970.

Hrushevsky, Mykhailo. *History of the Ukrainian Cossacks: From Pre-history to the Eleventh Century*, tr. Marta Skorupsky, ed. Andrzej Poppe, Edmonton and Toronto: Canadian Institute of Ukrainian Studies Press, 1997.

Imperiology: From Empirical Knowledge to Discussing Empire, 21st Century Slavic Eurasian Studies, no. 13, Sapporo: Slavic Research Center, 2007.

Kasten, Erich (ed.). *Pathways to Reform in Post-Soviet Siberia*, vol. 2, entitled *Properties as Culture—Culture as Property,* Berlin: Dietrich Reimar Verlag, 2005.

Khazanov, Anatoly M. and Andre Wink (eds). *Nomads in the Sedentary World*, Richmond, Surrey: Curzon Press, 2001.

Khodarkovsky, Mikhail. *Russia's Steppe Frontier: The Making of a Colonial Empire, 1500-1800*, Bloomington: Indiana University Press, 2002.

Kotkin, Stephen and David Wolff (eds). *Rediscovering Russia in Asia: Siberia and the Russian Far East*, Armonk: M.E. Sharpe, 1995.

Lamb, Harold. *Wolf of the Steppe: The Complete Cossack Adventures,* Howard Andrew Jones (ed.), Lincoln: University of Nebraska, 2006.

Lieven, Dominic. *Empire: The Russian Empire and its Rivals*, London: John Murray, 2000.

Lincoln, W. Bruce. *The Conquest of a Continent: Siberia and the Russians*, New York: Random House, 1994.

Marks, Steven G. *Road to Power: The Trans-Siberian Railroad and the Colonization of Asian Russia*, Ithaca: Cornell University Press, 1991.

Martin, Virginia. *Law and Custom in the Steppe: The Kazakhs of the Middle Horde and Russian Colonialism in the Nineteenth Century*, Richmond, Surrey: Curzon, 2001.

McNeill, William H. *Europe's Steppe Frontier, 1500-1800*, Chicago: University of Chicago Press, 1964.

Mazour, Anatole G. *Modern Russian Historiography* (rev. edn.), Westport, Connecticut: Greenwood Press, 1975.

——. *The Writing of History in the Soviet Union*, Stanford: Hoover Institution Press, 1971.

Naumov, Igor V. *The History of Siberia* (ed. David Collins), London: Routledge, 2006.

Newby, Eric. *The Big Red Train Ride*, London: Picador, 1978.

Novomeiskii, M.A. *My Siberian Life*, tr. A. Brown, London: Max Parrish, 1956.

Olcott, Martha Brill. *The Kazakhs*, Stanford: Hoover Institution Press, 1987.

Power, Daniel and Naomi Standen (eds). *Frontiers in Question: Eurasian Borderlands, 700-1700*, St. Martin's Press, 1999.

Privratsky, Bruce G. *Muslim Turkistan: Kazak Religion and Collective Memory*, Richmond, Surrey: Curzon, 2001.

Rasputin, Valentin. *Siberia, Siberia* [tr. with an introduction by Margaret Winchell and Gerald Mikkelsen], Evanston, Illinois: Northwestern University Press, 1996.

Rossabi, Morris. *China and Inner Asia: From 1368 to the Present Day*, New York: Pica Press, 1975.

Rourke, Shane O'. *The Cossacks*, Manchester: Manchester University Press, 2007.

Roy, Olivier. *The New Central Asia: The Creation of Nations*, London: I.B. Tauris, 2000.

Rudelson, Justin J. *Oasis Identities: Uyghur Nationalism Along China's Silk Road*, New York: Columbia University Press, 1997.

Sabol, Steven. *Russian Colonization and the Genesis of Kazak National Consciousness*, Houndmills, Basingstoke: Palgrave, Macmillan, 2003.

Sinor, Denis. *The Cambridge History of Early Inner Asia*, Cambridge: Cambridge University Press, 1990.

Toynbee, Sir Arnold Joseph. *A Study of History* (12 vols.), London: Oxford University Press, 1940.

Treadgold, Donald. *The Great Siberian Migration*, Princeton: Princeton University Press, 1957.

Witzenrath, Christoph. *Cossacks and the Russian Empire, 1598-1725: Manipulation, Rebellion and Expansion into Siberia*, London: Routledge, 2007.

Wood, Alan and R.A. French (eds.). *The Development of Siberia: People and Resources*, Basingstoke, Hampshire, England: Macmillan, 1989.

In Russian

Ablazhei, N.N. *Sibirs'koe oblastnichestvo v emigratsii*, Novosibirsk: Institute of Archaeology and Ethnography RAN, 2003.

Aktual'nye problemy sovremennovo Uygurovedeniya (Materialy mezhdunarodnoi konferentsii posvyaschennoy 50-letniyu Uygurovedeniya v Kazakhstane), Almaty, 2002.

Ananyev, D.A. et al., *"Novye Zemli" i osvoennie Sibri v XVII-XIX veke: ocherki istorii I istoriografii*, Novosibirsk, 2006.

Asfendiarov, Sandzhar. *Istoriia Kazakstana (s drevneishikh vremen)*, Alma Ata, 1935.

Lichnost' v istorii Sibiri, XVIII-XX vekov, Novosibirsk, 2007.

Masanov, N.E. et al., *Istoriya Kazakhstana, narody i kultury*, Almaty: Daik Press, 2001.

Rezun, D. Ya. *Frontir v istorii sibiri I severnoi Ameriki v XVII-XX vekov: obschee I osobennoe*, Vypusk 3, Novosibirsk, 2003.

Shilovskii, M.V. *Sibirskoe oblastnichestvo v obshchestvenno-politicheskoi zhizni regiona vo vtoroi polovine XIX-pervoi chetverti XX veke*, Novosibirsk: Institut Istorii SO RAN, 2008.

Shishkin, V.I. (ed.). *Aktual'nye problemy istorii sovetskoi Sibirii, sbornik nauchnovo trudov*, Novosibirsk: Institut Istorii SO RAN, 1990.

Tkachenko, V. Ya. and B.P. Pertsev. *Sukhoputnyi transport Sibiri: formirivanie opornoi seti zheleznykh I avtomobil'nykh dorog*, Novosibirsk: Institut Istorii SO RAN, 2003.

Tolybekov, S.E. *Kochevoe Obshchestvo kazakov v XVII-nachale XX veka: politico-ekonomicheskii analiz*, Alma Ata: Izdatel'stvo Nauka, Kazakhskoi SSR, 1971.

Viatkin, M. *Ocherki po istorii Kazakhskoi SSSR do drevneishykh vremen po 1870 gody*, Tom pervyi, Ogiz Gospolitizdat, 1941.

II. Articles

In English

Amanzhalova, Dina. 'The Movement for Siberian Regional and National Autonomy in the Early 1920s', *Sibirica*, 3, no. 1, 2003.

Banerjee, Anindita. 'The Trans-Siberian Railroad and Russia's Asia: Literature, Geopolitics, Philosophy of History', *Clio*, 34, 1: 2, 2004-5.

Bassin, Mark. 'The Russian Geographical Society, the "Amur Epoch", and the Great Siberian Expedition 1855-1863', *Annals of the Association of American Geographers*, 73 (2), 1983.

Brubaker, Rogers. 'Nationhood and National Question in the Soviet Union and Post-Soviet Eurasia: an Institutionalist Account', *Theory and Society*, 23 (1), 1994.

Busygina, Irina.'Russia's Regions in Search of Identity', *Acta Slavica Iaponica*, Issue 19, 2002.

Cesaro, M. Cristina. 'Walking a Tightrope: A Quest for Uyghur Identity', in Giampiero Bellingeri and Giovanni Pedrini (eds.), *Central Asia: A Decade of Reforms, Centuries of Memories*, Venice: Dipartimento do Studi Eurasiatici, Universita Ca' Foscari di Venezia, 2004.

Christian, David. 'Inner Eurasia as a Unit of World History', *Journal of World History*, 1994.

Collins, David. 'Russia's Conquest of Siberia: Evolving Russian and Soviet Historical Interpretations', *European Studies Review*, 12(1), 1982.

Darieva, Tsypylma. 'Recruiting for the Nation: Post-Soviet Transnational Migrants in Germany and Kazakhstan', in Erich Kasten (ed.), *Rebuilding Identities: Pathways to Reform in Post-Soviet Siberia*, Berlin: Dietrich Reimar Verlag, 2005.

David-Fox, Michael, Peter Holquist and Alexander M. Martin. 'The Imperial Turn', *Kritika*, vol. 7, no. 4, Fall 2006.

Diment, Galya. 'Exiled *from* Siberia: The Construction of Siberian Experience by Early Nineteenth Century Irkutsk Writers', in Galya Diment and Yuri Slezkine (eds.), *Between Heaven and Hell: The Myth of Siberia in Russian Culture*, New York: St. Martin's Press, 1993.

Eitzen, Hilda. 'Refiguring Ethnicity Through Conflicting Genealogies', *Nationalities Papers*, 26 (3), 1998.

Finke, Peter. 'Changing Property Rights System in Mongolia', *Max Planck Institute for Social Anthropology Working Papers*, Working Paper, no. 3, Halle/Salle 2000.

Frank, Allen. 'Islamic Transformation on the Kazakh Steppe, 1742-1917: Toward an Islamic History of Kazakhstan under Russian Rule', in Hayashi Tadayuki (ed.), *The Construction and Deconstruction of National Histories of Slavic Eurasia* [Proceedings of International Symposium held in Hokkaido, 10-13 July 2002], Sapporo: Slavic Research Center, Hokkaido University, 2003.

Gerhard, Dietrich. 'The Frontier in Comparative View', *Comparative Studies in Society and History*, vol. 1, no. 3, March 1959.

Gladney, Dru. 'Relational Alterity: Constructing Dungan (Hui), Uygur, and Kazakh Identities Across China, Central Asia and Turkey', *History and Anthropology*, 9 (4), 1996.

Glatter, Pete. 'Continuity and Change in the Tyumen Regional Elite 1991-2001', *Europe-Asia Studies*, vol. 55, no. 3, 2003.

Goryushkin, Leonid M. 'Migration, Settlement and the Rural Economy of Siberia, 1861-1914', in Alan Wood (ed.), *The History of Siberia: From Russian Conquest to Revolution*, London: Routledge, 1991.

Habeck, Joachim Otto. 'Dimensions of Identity', in Erich Kasten (ed.), *Rebuilding Identities: Pathways to Reform in Post-Soviet Siberia*, Berlin: Dietrich Reimar Verlag, 2005.

Hirsch, Francine. 'Getting to Know "The Peoples of the USSR": Ethnographic Exhibits as Soviet Virtual Tourism, 1923-34', *Slavic Review*, vol. 62, no. 4 [Tourism and Travel in Russia and the Soviet Union], Winter 2003.

Holl, Bruce T. 'Avvakum and the Genesis of Siberian Literature', in Galya Diment and Yuri Slezkine (eds.), *Between Heaven and Hell: The Myth of Siberia in Russian Culture*, New York: St. Martin's Press, 1993.

Hosking, Geoffrey. 'The Twentieth Century: In Search of New Ways, 1953-80', in Charles A. Moser (ed.), *The Cambridge History of Russian Literature*, Cambridge: Cambridge University Press, 1989.

Hughes, J.R. 'The Irkutsk Affair: Stalin, Siberian Politics and the End', *Soviet Studies*, vol. 41, no. 2, April 1989.

Ieda, Osama. 'Regional Identities and Meso-Mega Area Dynamics in Slavic Eurasia: Focussed on Eastern Europe', in Kimitaka

Matsuzato (ed.), *Emerging Meso-Areas in the Former Socialist Countries: Histories Revived or Improvised?*, Sapporo: Slavic Research Center, Hokkaido University, 2005.

Kappeler, Andreas. 'The Russian Empire and its Nationalities in Post-Soviet Historiographies', in Hayashi Tadayuki (ed.), *The Construction and Deconstruction of National Histories in Slavic Eurasia* [Proceedings of International Symposium held in Hokkaido, 10-13 July 2002], Sapporo: Slavic Research Center, Hokkaido University, 2003.

Kazymzhanov, Agyn Khairullovich and Keith Owen Tribble, 'The Political Tradition of the Steppe', *Nationalities Papers*, 26 (3), 1998.

Kerner, Robert Joseph. 'The Russian Eastward Movement: Some Observations on its Historical Significance', *Pacific Historical Review*, vol. XVII, no. 2, May 1948.

Koigeldiev, Mambet. 'The Alash Movement and the Soviet Government: A Difference of Positions', Uyama Tomohiko (ed.), *Empire, Islam and Politics in Central Asia*, Sapporo: Slavic Research Centre, Hokkaido University, 2007.

Kotkin, Stephen. 'Mongol Commonwealth? Exchange and Governance across the post-Mongol Space', *Kritika: Explorations in Russian and Eurasian History*, vol. 8, no. 3, Summer 2007.

Kovalaschina, Elena. 'The Historical and Cultural Ideals of the Siberian *Oblastnichestvo*', *Sibirica*, 6, Issue 2 (Autumn 2007).

Kreindler, Isabelle. 'Ibrahim Altynsaryn, Nikolai Ilminskii and the Kazakh National Awakening', *Central Asian Survey*, 2 (3), 1983.

Lattimore, Owen. 'At the Crossroads of Inner Asia', *Pacific Affairs*, vol. 23, no. 1, March 1950.

Lonsdale, Richard E. 'Siberian Industry Before 1917: The Example of Tomsk Guberniya', *Annals of the Association of American Geographers*, vol. 53, no. 4, December 1963.

McKenzie, Kermit E. 'Chokan Valikhanov: Kazakh Princeling and Scholar', *Central Asian Survey*, 8 (3), 1989.

Melvin, Neil J. 'The Consolidation of a New Regional Elite: The Case of Omsk 1987-1995', *Europe-Asia Studies*, vol. 50, no. 4, 1998.

Mogilner, Marina. 'The Most European Science in Russia: Defining the Empire Anthropologically', Kimitaka Matsuzato (ed.), *Emerging Meso Areas in the Former Socialist Countries: Histories*

Revived or Improvised?, Sapporo: Slavic Research Center, Hokkaido University, 2005.

Morgan, David. 'The Great "Yasa" of Chingiz Khan and the Mongol Ilkhanate', *Bulletin of the School of Oriental and African Studies*, University of London, vol. 49, no. 1, in Honour of Ann K.S. Lambton, 1986.

——. 'The "Great *Yasa* of Chinggis Khan" revisited', in Reuven Amitai and Michael Brian (eds.), *Mongols, Turks and Others: Eurasian nomads and the Sedentary World*, Leiden: Brill and Boston, 2005.

Moon, David. 'Peasant Migration and the Settlement of Russia's Frontiers, 1550-1897', *The Historical Journal*, 40 (4), 1997.

Norihiro, Naganawa. 'Molding the Muslim Community Through Tsarist Administration: *Mahalla* under the jurisdiction of the Orenburg Muhammedan Spiritual Assembly after 1905', *Acta Slavica Iaponica*, vol. 23, 2006.

Otarbayeva, Bakhytnur. 'A Brief History of the Kazak People', *Nationalities Papers*, 26 (3), 1998.

Pallot, J. 'The Development of Peasant Landholding: From Emancipation to the Revolution', James H. Bater and R.A. French (eds.), *Studies in Russian Historical Geography*, vol. 1, London: Academic Press, 1983.

Papava, Vladimir. 'Central Caucasasia Instead of Central Eurasia', *Central Asia and the Caucasus*, no. 2 (50), 2008.

Peyrose, Sebastien. 'The "Imperial Minority": An Interpretative Framework of the Russians in Kazakhstan in the 1990s', *Nationalities Papers*, vol. 36, no. 1, March 2008.

'Probing the Limits of Historical Metanarratives: Imperial Boundaries' [Editorial], *Ab Imperio*, 1, 2003.

Rieber, Alfred. 'Changing Concepts and Constructions of Frontiers: A Comparative Historical Approach', in *Ab Imperio*, no. 1, 2003.

Rigi, Jakob. 'Homeland as a Domestic Sphere in Kazakhstan: Historical Homeland (Istoricheskie Rodina), Homeland (Rodina) and Soviet Homeland (Sovietskoe Rodina), in Michael Gervers, Uradyn E. Bulag and Gillian Long (eds.), *History and Society in Central and Inner Asia*, Toronto: Toronto Studies in Central and Inner Asia, no. 7, 2005.

Roberts, Sean. 'The Uighurs of the Kazakh Borderlands: Migration and the Nation', *Nationalities Papers*, vol. 26, no. 3, 1998.

Rottier, Peter. 'The Kazakhness of Sedentarization: Promoting Progress as Tradition in Response to the Land Problem', *Central Asian Survey*, 22 (1), March 2003.

Rowe, William T. 'Owen Lattimore, Asia and Comparative History', *The Journal of Asian Studies*, vol. 66, no. 3 (August), 2007.

——. 'Approaches to Modern Chinese Social History', in Olivier Zunz (ed.), *Reliving the Past: The Worlds of Social History*, Chapel Hill: University of North Carolina Press, 1985.

Sabol, Steven. 'Kazak Resistance to Russian Colonization: Interpreting the Kenesary Kasymov Revolt, 1837-47', *Central Asian Survey*, June/September 2003.

Sautman, Barry. 'Preferential Policies for Ethnic Minorities in China: The Case of Xinjiang', William Safran (ed.), *National and Ethnoregional Identities in China*, London: Frank Cass Publishers, 1998.

Serebrennikov, I.I. 'The Siberian Autonomous Movement and its Future', *The Pacific Historical Review*, vol. 3, no. 4, December 1934.

Shishkin, Vladimir I. 'State Administration of Siberia from the End of the Nineteenth to the First Third of the Twentieth Centuries', *Regions: A Prism to View the Slavic Eurasian World, Towards a Discipline of Regionology*, Sapporo: Slavic Research Center, Hokkaido University, 2000.

Shukshin, Vasily. 'I Want to Live', *Soviet Literature* (1966), [tr.]. Website: www.sovlit.com/rasskazy/iwanttolive.html

Skubnevskii, V.A. and Iu. M. Goncharov, 'Siberian Merchants in the Latter Half of the Nineteenth Century', *Sibirica*, vol. 2, no. 1, April 2002.

Stebelsky, I. 'Agriculture and Soil Erosion in the European Forest-steppe', in James H. Bater and R.A. French (eds.), *Studies in Russian Historical Geography*, vol. 1, London: Academic Press, 1983.

——. 'The Frontier in Central Asia', James H. Bater and R.A. French (eds), *Studies in Russian Historical Geography*, vol. 1, London: Academic Press, 1983.

Sunderland, Willard. 'Peasant Pioneering: Russian Peasant Settlers Describe Colonization and the Eastern Frontier, 1880s-1910', *Journal of Social History*, Summer 2001.

Tohidi, Nayareh. 'Guardians of the Nation: Women, Islam and Soviet Legacy of Modernization in Azerbaijan', in Herbery L. Bodman and Nayereh Tohidi (eds.), *Women in Muslim Societies: Diversity within Unity*, Boulder, CO: Lynne Reiner Publications, 1998.

Tolmacheva, Marina. 'The Early Russian Exploration and Mapping of the Chinese Frontier', *Cahiers du Monde russe*, 41/1, janvier-mars 2000.

Tomilov, Nikolai. 'Ethnic Processes within the Turkic Population of the West Siberian Plain (sixteenth-twentieth centuries),' *Cahiers du monde russe*, 41/2-3, Avril-septembre 2000.

Tomohiko, Uyama. 'A Strategic Alliance between Kazakh Intellectuals and Russian Administrators: Imagined Communities in Dala Walayatining Gazeti (1888-1902)', in Hayashi Tadayuki (ed.), *The Construction and Deconstruction of National Histories in Slavic Eurasia*, Sapporo: Slavic Research Center, Hokkaido University, 2003.

——. '"Devotion to the People" and Paternalistic Authoritarianism Among Qazaq Intellectuals, from the Mid-nineteenth Century to 1917', in Stephane A. Dudoignon (ed.), *Devout Societies vs. impious states?: Transmitting Islamic Learning in Russia, Central Asia and China Through the Twentieth Century*, (Proceedings of an international colloquium held in the Carre des Sciences, French Ministry of Research, Paris, 12-13 November 2001), Berlin: Klaus Schwarz Verlag, 2004.

——.'The Geography of Civilizations: A Spatial Analysis of the Kazakh Intelligentsia's Activities, from the mid-19th Century to the Early 20th Century', in Kimitaka Matsuzato (ed.), *Regions: A Prism to View the Slavic Eurasian World: Towards a Discipline of Regionology*, Sapporo: Slavic Research Center, Hokkaido University, 2000.

Trofimenko, Henry. 'Long-term Trends in the Asia-Pacific Region: A Soviet Evaluation', *Asian Survey*, vol. 29, no. 3, March 1989.

Varneck, Elena. 'Siberian Native Peoples after the February Revolution', *Slavonic and East European Review*, vol. 2, no. 1, March 1943.

Weiss, Claudia. 'Representing the Empire: The Meaning of Siberia for Russian Imperial Identity', *Nationalities Papers* 35, no. 3 (July 2007).

Wertheim, Suzanne. 'Language Ideologies and the Purification of post-Soviet Tatar', *Ab Imperio*, 1, 2003.

Yorke, Andrew. 'Business and Politics in Krasnoyarsk *Krai*', *Europe-Asia Studies*, vol. 55, no. 2, 2003.

Zweynert, Joachim. 'Economic Ideas and Institutional Change: Evidence from Soviet Economic Debates 1987-1991', *Europe-Asia Studies*, vol. 58, no. 2, March 2006.

In Russian

Abashin, Sergei. 'Arkhaeologia sredneaziatskikh natsionalizmov', *Ab Imperio*, 1, 2003.

Aleksandrov, V.A. 'Voisko-organizatsiya sibirskikh sluzhylykh lyudei XVII veka', *Istoriya SSSR*, no. 3, 1988.

Amanzhalova, Dina. 'Kazakhskaia avtonomiia: ot zamysla natsionalov k samoopredeleniyu po-Sovietski', *Acta Slavica Iaponica*, vol. 21, 2004.

Bezvikonnaia, Elena. 'Geopoliticheskoe prostranstvo stepnovo kraia: Omskaia oblast' I problema granitsii v gosudarstvennom strotel'stve Rossiskoi imperii (20-30 gody XIX veke), *Ab Imperio*, 1, 2003.

Kappeler, Andreas. 'Yuzhniy I vostochnyi frontir Rossii', *Ab Imperio*, no. 1, 2003.

Laitin, David. 'Chto takoe yazykovoe soobshchestvo?', *Ab Imperio*, 1, 2003.

Mamisk, T.S. 'Povo'lzhe I Priob'e:Ochagi rannevo kulturnovo vzaimodeistviya, XVII-seredina XIX vek', *Sibirskii plavil'ny kotel: sotsial'no-demograficheskie protsessi v Severnoi Azii XVI-nachala XX veka, Sbornik nauchnoi statei*, Novosibirsk, 2004.

Nikitin, N.E. 'Voennosluzhiliye lyudi I Sibiri v XVII veke', *Istoriya SSSR*, no. 2, 1980.

Shilovsky, M.V. 'Sibirskii frontir: neokonchennoe puteshestvie po neizveddanoi zemle', *Evraziia: regionalnye perspektivy: sbornik materialov mezhdunarodnoi nauchnoi konferentsii 1-4 Iuniya 2007godu*, Novosibirsk: Sibirskoe Nauchnoe Izdatel'stvo, 2007.

——. 'Frontir i pereseleniya', *Frontir I istorii Sibirii I severnoi Ameriki v 17-20 vekov: obshchee I osobennoe, Sbornik nauchnoi statei*, Novosibirsk, 2003.

Skrynnikova, Tatyana. 'Rossiya v samoidentifikatsii Buryat', *Ab Imperio*, no. 1, 2003.

Trepavlov, Vadim.'Altytuly: ostatki Nogaiskoi ordy v kazakhskikh stepyakh', *Viestnikh Evrazii*, no. 2 (13), 2001.

Yanovskii, N. *Pisateli Sibiri (izbrannie stati),* Chapter 'Vernye Syny Sibiri' ['Proza I poeziya N.M. Yadrintseva', 'O vospominanyakh G.N. Potanina'], Moscow: Sovremennik, 1988.

III. Bibliographies

Central Eurasian Reader: A Biennial Journal of Critical Bibliography and Epistemology of Central Eurasian Studies, Berlin: Klaus Schwarz Verlag, 1, 2008.

Dudoignon, Stephane A. and Hisao Komatsu. *Research Trends in Modern Central Eurasian Studies (18th-20th Centuries): A Selective and Critical Bibliography of Works Published between 1985 and 2000, Parts I & II.* Tokyo: The Toyo Bunko, 2003 and 2006.

IV. Reviews

Baron, Nick. 'New Spatial Histories of 20th century Russia and the Soviet Union: Exploring the Terrain' [review of Evgeny Dobrenko and Eric Naiman (eds), *The Landscape of Stalinism: The Art and Ideology of Soviet Space,* Seattle: University of Washington Press, 2003; Karl Schoegel's *Im Raume Lesen Wir die Zeit: Uber Zivilisationsgeschichte und Geopolitik,* Munich: Carl Hanser Verlag, 2003; Emma Widdis, *Visions of a New Land: Soviet Film from the Revolution to the Second World War,* New Haven: Yale University Press, 2003], *Kritika: Explorations in Russian and Eurasian History,* 9, 2, Spring 2008.

Cosmo, Nicola Di. 'New Directions in Inner Asian History: A Review Article' [review of Thomas Allsen's *Commodity and Exchange in the Mongol Empire: A Cultural History of Islamic Textiles,* Cambridge University Press, 1997; Jorg Michael Scheil's *Die chinesischen vertragsurkunden aus Turfan,* Franz Steiner, 1995; Jenny F. SO and Emma C. Bunker's *Traders and Raiders on China's Northern Frontier,* University of Washington Press and Arthur Sackler Gallery, 1995], *JESHO,* 42 (2), 1999.

Hagen, Mark von. [Review of Wolfgang Faust's monograph *Russlands Goldener Boden: Der sibirche regionalismus in der zweiten halfte des 19 Jahnhunderts,* Cologne: Bohlau, 1980], *Russian Review,* vol. 41, no. 1, January 1982.

——. 'Empires, Borderlands and Diasporas: Eurasia as anti-paradigm for the Post-Soviet era', *The American Historical Review*, vol. 109, no. 2, April 2004.

Hamburg, G.M. 'Imperial Entanglements: Two New Histories of Russia's Western and Southern Borderlands' [review of Robert D. Crews', *For Prophet and Tsar: Islam and Empire in Russia and Central Asia*, Cambridge, MA: Harvard University Press, 2006; Mikhail Dmitrievich Dolbilov and Aleksei Il'ich Miller, *Zapadnye okrainy Rossiskoi imperii*, Moscow: Novoe Literaturnow Obozrenie, 2006], *Kritika*, vol. 9, no. 2, Spring 2008.

Taylor, Patrick R. [review of S.A. Krasil'nikov and V.L. Soskin, *Intelligentsia Sibiri v period borby za pobedu I utverzhdenie Sovetskoi vlasti (1917-leto 1918)], The American Historical Review*, vol. 92, no. 4, October 1987.

Wood, Alan. 'Leonid Mikhailovich Goryushkin (1927-1999)', [obituary], *Sibirica*, vol. 2, no. 1, April 2002.

V. Websites

http://oblastnichestvo.lib.tomsk.ru/page.php?id=2

www.zaimka.ru.

http://xroads.virginia.edu/~Hyper/TURNER.

Index